THE LIFE AND TIMES

OF

SIR PHILIP SIDNEY.

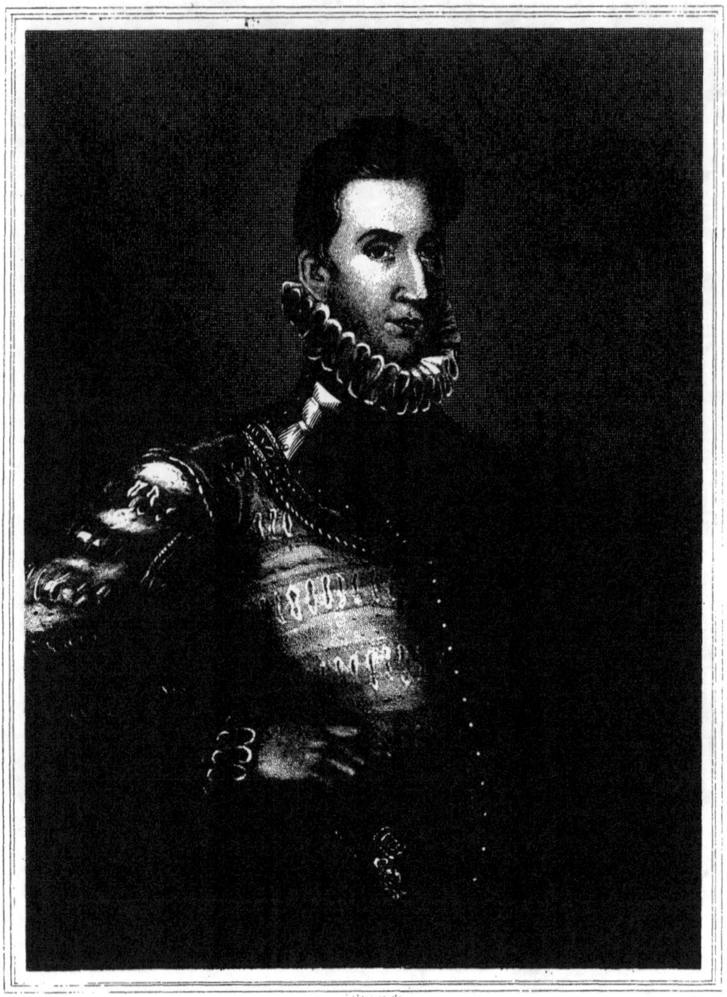

J. Glover sc.

SIR PHILIP SIDNEY.

OB. 1586.

FROM THE ORIGINAL OF SIR ANT. MORE IN THE COLLECTION OF

HIS GRACE THE DUKE OF [illegible]

THE LIFE AND TIMES

OF

SIR PHILIP SIDNEY.

> "Sidney, as he fought
> And as he fell, and as he lived and loved,
> Sublimely mild, a Spirit without spot,
> Arose"
>
> SHELLEY'S ADONAIS.

THIRD EDITION.

BOSTON:
TICKNOR AND FIELDS.
M DCCC LIX.

RIVERSIDE, CAMBRIDGE:
STEREOTYPED AND PRINTED BY
H. O. HOUGHTON AND COMPANY

FROM THE AUTHOR.

THE only noted memoirs of Sir PHILIP SIDNEY are those written by Fulke Greville and by Dr. Zouch. The former, although the work of a contemporary, and a personal friend, is painfully meagre; the latter, though sufficiently voluminous, is incomplete; and both, being out of print, are be yond the reach of ordinary readers. The lives prefixed by Gray to Sidney's Sonnets, and by Pears to the Correspondence of Languet; the ſketches contained in Lodge's "Portraits of Illuſtrious Personages," in Lloyd's "Statesmen and Favorites," in the "Britiſh Bibliographer," "The Biographia Britannica," and several papers on the same theme in the Engliſh Reviews, are interesting and valuable, but neceſſarily deficient in fulness and continuity. I have here endeavored to collect the scattered souvenirs of Sidney's life; to verify every recorded fact, and to exclude every fiction, however plauſible, which, while gilding the ſtory with false attractions, would mar the higher beauty that belongs to truth.

If this little volume, which is the fruit of leisure hours, and of an earneſt admiration of its subject, ſhall afford information or intereſt to its readers, I ſhall willingly endure the criticisms to which it is liable ; conscious that, while abler pens might give a greater charm to the annals of the illuſtrious Sidney, I have at leaſt aimed to present them with clearness and ſimplicity, and without pretence.

S. M. D.

Oct. 1858.

TO MY SON

I DEDICATE THIS MEMORIAL, OF ONE WHOSE NAME IS A SYNONYM FOR EVERY MANLY VIRTUE, AND WHOSE EXAMPLE, SURPASSING THE STANDARD OF THE AGE WHICH IT ADORNED, REMAINS STILL BRILLIANT WHEN CENTURIES HAVE PASSED AWAY.

PENSHURST CASTLE.

Kent.

THE LIFE AND TIMES

OF

SIR PHILIP SIDNEY.

CHAPTER I.

IN the queenly days of Elizabeth, the soil of England was trodden by noble men, whose footprints will be revered until the sun shall gild for the last time the dominions on which it has been said, he never sets. Bacon, who has left a legacy of wisdom quite large enough to redeem his meanness; Burleigh, the serene, sagacious statesman; Sir Walter Raleigh, the mirror of chivalrous accomplishment; Sir Francis Drake, the renowned navigator; Howard, the brave Earl of Effingham, whose fleet defeated the Spanish Armada; Spenser, Shakspeare, and a host of minor lights, glittered in the firmament of the august Tudor. No other annals of sovereignty can boast such an assemblage of learning, wit, enterprise, statesmanship, and courtly grace; for to her satellites, rather than to herself, belong the registered glories of Elizabeth's reign.

Amidst those unforgotten heroes of an almost forgotten day, stands one whose brief and beautiful life was pronounced by Campbell, "poetry put into action"—a hero born to greatness, achieving greatness, and having greatness thrust upon him; not the greatness of massive intellect or of hereditary position, but rather that which is the result of a perfectly harmonious nature; the union of inherited talent and rare culture, with a heart spontaneously generous, earnest, and true. When we add to this the personal endowments of manly beauty, of stately presence, and of gentle speech, we may not marvel that he was the cynosure of the court and the idol of friendship; that the partial queen claimed him as "her jewel," or that famous men sought posthumous praise in the monumental record, "The friend of SIR PHILIP SIDNEY."

It is to be regretted that the memorials of this illustrious favorite are so brief and scanty, especially those of his social and domestic relations. Scarcely an anecdote of his private life has been transmitted for the benefit of those curious to know just how the "hero" appeared to his *valet de chambre*. But since no picture is preserved of him in dressing-gown and slippered *negligé*, we are fain to content ourselves with such gala-draped sketches as we can find, believing, too, that the inner life is often revealed through the fluttering of state robes.

The castle of Penshurst situated in the county of Kent, was the baronial dwelling of the Sidney family, though, long before their name was known beyond the shores of France, its massive towers and embattled front had frowned on many a feudal lord and rude retainer. Ben Jonson's verse brings back to us the echoing sounds of its departed glory—

"Thou art not, Penshurst, built to envious show
Of touch or marble; nor canst boast a row
Of polish'd pillars, or a roofe of gold;
Thou hast no lantherne, whereof tales are told,
Or stayre, or courts; but stand'st an ancient pile,
And these grudg'd at, art reverenced the while,
Thou ioy'st in better markes, of soyle, of ayre,
Of wood, of water; therein thou art faire;
Thou hast thy walkes for health as well as sport;
Thy *Mount*, to which the *Dryads* doe resort;
Where Pan and Bacchus, their high feasts have made,
Beneath the broad beech and the chest-nut shade;
That taller tree, which of a nut was set
At his great birth, where all the *Muses* met."

The principal buildings in this ancient pile form

a quadrangle enclosing a spacious court. Over the grand portal was an inscription testifying that the manor was a gift from Edward the Sixth to William de Sidney, who was his tutor, chamberlain, and steward of his household, and had been distinguished by his bravery on the field of Flodden.

The great banqueting hall was curiously decorated with grotesque figures that supported the roof, and its fireplace, encased in a frame of iron, is said to have had strength and capacity enough to hold huge piles of wood, and nearly sufficient to sustain the trunk of a giant tree. The stairs were formed of vast blocks of solid oak, and the floors of many of the state apartments were of massive planks from the same royal wood. The spacious portrait gallery was, in the latter part of the last century, adorned with curious and rare historical pictures, and also with portraits, some of them by Holbein, of the Sidneys and Dudleys, and of the monarchs who were their friends and patrons. There were the "counterfeit presentments" of Sir Philip Sidney, and of his sister, the Countess of Pembroke, the subject of Jonson's noted epitaph:

> "Underneath this sable hearse,
> Lies the subject of all verse;

Sidney's sister, Pembroke's mother,
Death, ere thou hast slain another,
Learn'd and fair, and good as she,
Time shall throw his dart at thee," &c.

A portrait of their celebrated uncle, Robert Dudley, Earl of Leicester, was also then a tenant of that voiceless gallery. An epigram found in the Hawthornden MSS. is of a less flattering character:

"Here lies a valiant warrior,
Who never drew a sword.
Here lies a noble courtier
Who never kept his word.
Here lies the Earle of Léicester,
Who governed the Estates,
Whom the Earth could never living love,
And the just Heaven now hates."

Sweet Amy Robsart was better avenged by posterity than by her contemporaries. The proud peer, whose art kept pace with his ambition, whose guile was equalled only by his guilt, whose vanity instructed his revenge, who poisoned with the unhesitating skill of a Borgia, and with the precaution of a Catiline kept ever near him the instruments for every species of sin, might well defy both scrutiny and retribution, under the protecting partiality of an enamored queen. But the fair young wife was displaced in vain, for in Elizabeth's heart the rule of love always yielded eventually to the love of rule, and Leicester was left with that crime upon his conscience, without even the compensation of a crown upon his head.

The Sidneys were an ancient and honorable family, of French origin, their lineal ancestor having accompanied Henry the Second from Anjou, and afterwards attended him as one of his chamberlains. But we hear little of them until the services of Sir William, in the fleets and armies of Henry the Eighth, obtained for him the grant of Penshurst Castle. His only son Henry, the father of Sir Philip, was the most intimate friend of the good young king, Edward the Sixth, of whom Hooker said that "though he died young, he lived long, for life is in *action*." After the death of this lamented Prince, Sir Henry's abilities as a diplomatist and a statesman elicited the highest tokens of esteem from both Mary and Elizabeth. Historians have cited as one of the caprices of fame that the father should now be remembered through the son, rather than the son through the father. He was president of Wales and governor of Ireland, and in these difficult offices of trust, his integrity and philanthropy were preëminent. He softened the wild asperities of Wales by planting there the institutions of civilization, some vestiges of which yet remain. It was impossible to bring order out of the chaos of civil war and barbarism that had distracted unhappy Ireland for many centuries, but Sir Henry, having with Roman patriotism spent both life and fortune in the effort, gained, like Valerius, the meed of praise from the public voice, and of burial from the public purse.

England numbered, in that day, as many good and accomplished women, as brave and princely men; and not least among them was Mary, the wife of Sir Henry Sidney, and daughter of that unfortunate Duke of Northumberland, whose "vaulting ambition o'erleaped itself" in the vain attempt to enthrone Lady Jane Grey. The children of the Duke were of course implicated in his attainder, but from some anomalous impulse of goodness on the part of Philip Second of Spain, the clemency of his newly wedded Queen was solicited and obtained in behalf of all of them except Lord Guilford Dudley, the husband of Lady Jane. So unaccountable a departure from the usual Machiavelian policy of Philip, must either be considered a mistake, or attributed to a desire to court the regard of the people of England, who already looked upon him and upon his arrogant Spanish retinue with jealous eyes. The exemplary and amiable character of Lady Mary Sidney added grace to her own noble house of Dudley and another ornament to the annals of the lord of Penshurst. Her delicate sensibility of temperament and love of quiet and domestic life, led her to prefer the seclusion of her beautiful home to the glittering gayeties of the court. There she offered an asylum to such of her family as civil calamity had spared, and reared the children whose lives were the best tributes to her maternal worth.

The eldest son of these admirable parents was born on the 29th of November, 1554, during the reign of Queen Mary, who among other marks of her favor bestowed upon him the name of her renowned spouse. Happily the gift of a name does not imply the transmission of the qualities thereby represented, or the youthful Philip might well have demurred to the royal compliment. The mantle of that eminent bigot and illustrious brigand, cast no shadow upon either his character or his career.

His birth was poetically commemorated by the planting of an oak,

> "That taller tree which of a nut was set,"

and whose bravery of verdure overshadowed the park of Penshurst for nearly two centuries after its prototype had passed away.* Many years later, when the tenants came on gala days to greet their lord, they used to adorn themselves with boughs from this consecrated oak, in memory of Sir Philip.

His childhood and youth were marked by a singular love of learning, by a generous and amiable disposition, and by that pensive dignity of demeanor usually associated with high-toned and reflective minds. The patent of nobility was his, not only in social position but as the inalienable gift of nature. We may fancy his juvenile sports under the "broad beech and the chestnut shade," chasing the deer, practising simple feats of horsemanship, or tilting in mock tournaments; but evincing even then, it was said, thought beyond his years, and habits of

* "Sidney here was born;
Sidney, than whom no greater, braver man,
His own delightful genius ever feigned,
Illustrating the vales of Arcady,
With courteous courage, and with loyal loves.
Upon his natal day the acorn here
Was planted; it grew up a stately oak,
And in the beauty of its strength it stood
And flourished, when its perishable part
Had mouldered, dust to dust. That stately oak
Itself hath mouldered now, but Sidney's name
Endureth in his own immortal works."

SOUTHEY.

inquiry and observation that were the marvel of his teachers. Destined for the life of a courtier and a statesman, no pains were spared to fit him for distinction, not only as a brilliant, but as a good man. Letters in Latin and in French, written by him at the age of twelve years to his father, elicited a reply which is considered by all his biographers so fine a model of paternal advice that it may be worth while to insert it here. Through its quaint old Saxon is seen the most watchful care for the mental progress of his son, and for his culture of true religion—that which is of the fervent heart, rather than of the bended knee. It seems quite probable that this letter, which was preserved in the "Sidney Papers," may have been the source of suggestion to Sir Walter Raleigh, Sir Matthew Hale, and others, whose epistolary counsels to their children are still commended.

"I have reaceaved too letters from yow, one written in Latine, the other in French; which I take in goode parte, and will yow to exercise that practice of learninge often: for that will stand yow in moste steade, in that profession of lyf that yow are born to live in. And since this ys my first letter that ever I did write to yow, I will not that yt be all emptie of some advyses, which my naturall care of yow provokethe me to wish yow to foloye, as documents to yow in this your tendre age. Let yowr first actyon be the lyfting up of yowr mynd to Almighty God, by harty prayer; and felingly dysgest the woords yow speake in prayer, with contynual meditation and thinkinge of him to whom yow praye, and of the matter for which yow praye. And use this at an ordinarye hower. Whereby the time ytself will put yow in remembrance to doe that, which yow are accustomed to doe in that tyme. Apply yowr study to suche howres, as yowr discrete master dothe assign yow, earnestlye; and the time, I knowe, he will so lymitt, as shal be both sufficient for yowr learninge, and saf for yowr health. And mark the sens, and the matter of that yow read, as well as the woordes. So shal yow both enreiche yowr tonge with woordes, and yowr wytte with matter; and judgement will growe as yeares growyth in yow. Be humble and obedient to yowr master, for unless yow frame yowr selfe to obey others, yea, and feale in yowr selfe what obedience is, yow shall never be able to teach others how to obey yow. Be curteese of gesture, and affable to all men, with diversitee of reverence, according to the dignitie of the person. There ys nothing, that wynneth so much with so lytell cost. Use moderate dyet, so as after yowr meate, yow may find yowr wytte fresher and not duller, and yowr body more lyvely, and not more heavye. Seldom drinke wine, and yet sometimes doe, least, being enforced to drinke upon the sodayne, yow should find yowr selfe inflamed. Use exercise of bodye, but suche as ys without peryll of yowr yointes or bones. It will encrease yowr force, and enlardge yowr breathe. Delight to be cleanly, as well in all parts of yowr bodye, as in yowr garments. It shall make yow grateful in yche company, and otherwise lothsome. Give yowr selfe to be merye, for yow degenerate from yowr father, yf yow find not yowr selfe most able in wytte and bodye, to doe any thinge when yow be most merye; But let yowr myrthe be ever void of all scurilitee, and bitinge woordes to any man, for an wound given by a woorde is oftentimes harder to be cured, than that which is given with the sword. Be yow rather a herer, and bearer away of other men's talke, than a begynner or procurer of speeche, otherwise yow shall be counted to delight to hear yowr selfe speak. Yf yow heare a wise sentence, or an apt phrase, commytte yt to yowr memorye, with respect to the circumstance, when yow shal speake yt. Let never othe be hearde to come out of yowr mouthe, nor woord of ribaudrye; detest yt in others, so shal custome make to yowr selfe a lawe against yt in yowr selfe. Be modest in yche assemble, and rather be rebuked of light felowes for meden-like shamefastnes, than of yowr sad friends for pearte boldnes. Thinke upon every woorde that yow will speake, before yow utter hit, and remembre how nature hath rampared up, as yt were, the tonge with teeth, lippes, yea and hair without the lippes, and all betokening raynes or bridles, for the loose use of that membre. Above all things tell no untruthe, no not in trifels. The custome of hit is naughte, and let it not satisfie yow, that for a time, the hearers take yt for a truthe, for after yt will be known as yt is, to yowr shame; for ther cannot be a greater reproche to a gentellman than to be accounted a lyare. Study and endevour yowr selfe to be vertuously occupied. So shall yow make suchean habite of well doinge in yow, that yow shal not knowe how to do evell, thoughe you wold. Remember, my sonne, the noble blood yow are descended of, on yowr mother's side; and thinke that only, by vertuous lyf and good action, yow may be an ornament to that illustre famylie; and otherwise, through vice and slouthe, yow shall be counted *labes generis*, one of the greatest curses that can happen to man. Well, my littell Philippe, this is ynough for me, and to muche, I fear, for yow. But, yf I shall finde that this light meale of digestione nourishe any thing the weake stomake of yowr yonge capacitie, I will, as I find the same growe stronger, fead yt with toofer foode.

"Your lovinge father so long as yow live in
"the feare of God,
"H. SYDNEY.

If the spirit of prophecy had inspired this communication, it could not better have pictured the future character of young Sidney; and we are told that he was, even then, fondly called by his father "*lumen familiæ suæ*," the brightness of his household. Trinity College at Cambridge, and Christ Church at Oxford, were the arenas of his intellectual labors, and there, in the Olympic strife with the young and noble sons of England, he wore the laurels of success. Spencer, Raleigh, and the historians Camden and Carew, were among his fellow-students, and the latter has incidentally given us a glimpse of his own scholarship, and that of young Sidney. "Upon a wrong-conceived opinion touching my sufficiency, I was called to dispute *extempore* with the matchless Sir Philip Sidney, in presence of the Earls of Leicester and Warwick, and divers other great personages."* He early became a

* Old England's Worthies.

proficient in Latin and Greek, and especially delighted in research among curious old books and antique parchments, the exhumed mementoes of the past. The overhanging gloom of the dark ages had lately rolled away from the world of letters. Literature was no longer a costly myth, nor science the veiled mystery of the monk and the antiquary. The student might now light his midnight lamp by the rays of Homer, and drink from the sparkling fountains of Virgil. Plato belonged, not to Greece, but to the world, and the Peripatetic again walked the broad highway of common life. It was said of Philip Sidney, that "he cultivated not one art or science, but the whole circle of arts and sciences; his capacious and comprehensive mind aspiring to preëminence in every branch of knowledge." We may add his name to the chronicle of those who, in the flush of youth, have turned aside from the allurements of rank, of wealth, or of pleasure, to the

—"Fairy tales of science and the long result of Time,"

thus early witnessing the truth of Thierry's conclusion from a long life of varied experiment, "Believe me, there is no earthly happiness equal to the unceasing pursuit of knowledge."

Mirandola, an Italian nobleman who lived in

the fifteenth century, was the marvel of learned men and the pride of universities, and, like the "admirable Crichton," at the age of twenty-three he challenged the savants of Italy to enter the lists with him in public disputation. Pascal, who shone in goodness as in learning, having been forbidden by his father the use of mathematical books, was one day accidentally found sitting on the floor of his room, surrounded by charcoal diagrams; his irrepressible love of science having led him, untaught, to the exact demonstration of the thirty-second problem of Euclid. When only sixteen, he wrote so able a treatise on Conic Sections that it was attributed by Des Cartes to the labors of his father. Scaliger, who was deemed one of the most learned men of his age; Lipsius, the celebrated scholar and critic; Tasso, the hapless poet who

——" Wrecked on one slight bark
The prodigal treasures of his bankrupt soul;"

and Crichton himself, who, it was said, "wrote and spoke to perfection ten languages at the age of twenty," besides being well versed in general science;—of these, some walked the stage of Europe contemporaneously with Philip Sidney, and, like him, they all aimed in youth at a lofty mark. Talent may be late in its unfolding, but habits of industrious application, unless formed early are seldom formed at all.

"There is no such thing as genius," said Hogarth, two hundred years later; "genius is nothing but labor and diligence." Perhaps Hogarth's own creative abilities and acute intuitions falsified his assertion; but it also bears the high indorsement of Sir Isaac Newton, who declared that "if ever he had effected any thing, it had been by patient thinking." It was certainly rather through "labor and diligence" than from any transcendent native power, that our hero reaped his abundant harvest; and it is a significant tribute to the goodness of his heart and the charm of his manner, that his life, not only now, but to its lamented close, was unblighted by the attacks of envy and jealousy—those scoffing fiends that ever walk in the shadow of the successful, whether in social, intellectual, or political achievement.

Before he had laid aside the academic gown at the age of seventeen, the pioneers of invention and of discovery sought the aid of his discriminating judgment, and painters and musicians found in him a liberal and appreciative patron. Every hour had its earnest employment; but he had none to give to idle pleasures or to questionable indulgence. The kingdom of the Beautiful was his chosen home. On its heaven-touched heights, and by its pure streams, his young genius expanded its glorious capacities, sweeping with rapid wing the orbit of science, and soaring onward with untiring eye and yet loftier aim.

Like a light within a vase, the spirit shone through its outer temple. Tall and finely proportioned, with regular and handsome features, hair of the sunny hue that poets love,* and deep blue eyes, expressive of thought and feeling, Philip Sidney went forth into the world with every endowment that youth could covet,

——"Not mailed in scorn,
But in the armor of a pure intent."

Schiller says, "let no man measure by a scale of perfection the meagre products of reality." Since the best of men are still but men, it is perhaps a pity that the faults of this oft-named favorite, the shadows upon this luminous humanity, are not recorded for our criticism, and, we may add, for our encouragement. The Egyptian sculptors were forbidden to model their statues by their own

* "He was extremely beautiful," said the celebrated antiquary, John Aubrey; "he much resembled his sister, but his hair was not red, but a little inclining; viz: a dark amber color."

ideal creations, and compelled to adhere to the sacred measures of the priesthood. Like them we copy with literal chisel from biography and history, without improvising even a fancy to relieve the monotony of truth.

CHAPTER II.

IN all ages, and in all countries, whenever the love of action has triumphed over the love of repose, has been seen a curiosity to explore the recesses of nature, to examine the achievements of art, and to read the chequered tablets of man's life and character, as written in courts and in cottages, in palaces and in prisons; in the intrigues of governments, and the arcana of private life; in the cabinet of the minister who holds the helm of state; by the roadside stream, where the pilgrim eats his morning crust; in the studio of the artist, whose embodied visions of beauty speak to the responsive soul of universal humanity. To men of letters, travelling is a means of knowledge; to men of taste, of accomplishment; to the idle, a relief from ennui; to the busy, a rest from labor; to the sorrowful, a refuge from grief; to the joyful, a new field of enjoyment. At the period of which we write, the intercommunication of travel was far more restricted than at the present day, both by the physical impediments which science has since removed, and by the manifold jealous precautions which still bristled around countries but lately emerged from feudalism. The social maxim of Rochefoucault—"to treat every friend as if he might one day be an enemy"—seemed still to be the national and universal law of Europe. In England, the prestige and the privilege of foreign travel were obtained only by a special grant from the reigning sovereign, and generally awarded to none except merchants on business, to servants of the crown, and gentlemen of the realm. Those less fortunate subjects, who were condemned to remain within the sea-washed shores of their native land, had not even the modern consolation of books of adventure. The vivid panoramas of people and of places that now divest distance of its mysteries, bringing the Pyramids to our opera glasses, and the roar of Arctic waters to our very ear, were then unpictured for the home-sequestered millions.

We may imagine the hopes that brightened the eye of Philip Sidney, when, having bid adieu to the venerable cloisters of Oxford, he received a license from Queen Elizabeth "to go to parts beyond the sea for the space of two years, for his attaining the knowledge of foreign languages." A brilliant cortege departed from London on the 26th of May, 1572, and he was of the number, equipped, says the old historian, with three servants and four horses. The Earl of Lincoln, Admiral of the Sea, had lately been appointed Ambassador Extraordinary to France, and was attended thither by a numerous retinue of the chivalry of England.

The resident minister at the court of Charles IX. was at that time Sir Francis Walsingham, one of the most zealous, faithful, and successful of Elizabeth's statesmen; unimpeachable in private life, but liable, it must be admitted, to the imputation of unscrupulous artifice in the public service. To trample upon bigotry with yet greater bigotry, was the error of the age, and the one blot upon Walsingham's character. His almost puritanical zeal in the Protestant cause, deepened by exile in early life, led him to the employment of every snare and every intrigue that could bring disgrace and ruin to the disaffected Catholics. His eighteen spies, and fifty-three agents, who were but spies under a privileged name, haunted with ghostly omnipresence every court in Europe, while at home a system of social espionage, almost as efficient as that of Fouché, rendered him the very Nemesis of conspiracy and crime. The Queen was many times indebted for her life and her crown to that "eternal vigilance," which is the price of royal security as well as of republican liberty. One of his most subtle schemes was that which caused the detention for an entire year of the Spanish Armada in 1587. This magnificent flotilla, the marvel of Spain and the terror of Europe, was nearly prepared for its yet unknown destiny. Like a huge leviathan slumbering before its conflict with an angry sea, it reposed in the sunny waters of the harbor of Cadiz, waiting the hour and the command. In a private letter from Philip II. to the Pope, the blessing of his Holiness had been solicited upon the mysterious enterprise, whose object, the Spanish council were informed, should be disclosed on the courtier's return. The English minister having learned thus much, and probably feeling that in such a case "a *little* knowledge" was, if not a "dangerous," at least a useless, thing, determined to know more. Through another of his familiar spirits, a Venetian priest at Rome, a gentleman of the bedchamber of Sextus V. turned traitor to his trust. The keeper of the keys of St. Peter was one of the most acute and Argus-eyed of his order; but, forgetting on this occasion that his own keys were in unanointed hands, he carelessly slept while his cabinet was opened, and a copy hastily taken of the communication from his "dear and Catholic son." Walsingham was soon both forewarned and forearmed. His next step was to defeat the Spanish loan from the bank of Genoa, and thus from lack of funds the Armada was detained until the arrival (from America and the Indies) of an argosy which brought the needful supplies.*

An old writer † says of this subtle statesman,—"No one did better ken the Secretary's craft, to get counsels out of others, and keep them in himself. Marvellous his sagacity in examining suspected persons, either to make them confess the truth, or confound themselves by denying it to their detection . . . . Indeed, his simulation (which all allow lawful) was as like to dissimulation (condemned by all good men) as two things could be which were not the same. He thought that gold might, but intelligence could not, be bought too dear; the cause that so great a statesman left so small an estate, and so public a person was so privately buried in St. Paul's." It was indeed a disgrace to the parsimonious Queen, that this efficient and invaluable servant was during his long and anxious life most meagrely rewarded, and that his mortal remains were

* Lodge's Portraits of Illustrious Personages.

† Fuller's Worthies of England.

interred by his friends in the silence and secrecy of night, lest, in accordance with the custom of the times, they should be seized by his creditors. This was not, however, an uncommon illustration of what she termed her "great and inestimable care of her loving subjects."

To this distinguished man, then at the zenith of his career, Sidney was commended by the following letter from his uncle the Earl of Leicester:—

"MR. WALSINGHAM,

"For so much as my nephew Philip Sidney ys lycensed to travyle, and doth presentlie repayre unto those parts with my L. Admyrall, I have thought good to commend him by these my friendlie lines unto you, as to one I am well assured will have a speciall care of him during his abode there. He is young and rawe, and no doubt shall find those countries, and the demeanors of the people somewhat straunge unto him; in which respect your good advice and counsell shall greatlie behove him, for his better directions, which I do most heartilie pray you to voutsafe him, with any other friendlie assistance you shall think nedefull for him. His father and I do intend his further travalye, if the world be quiett, and you shall so think it convenient for him. I pray you we may be advertised thereof, to the end the same his travalye may be therefore directed accordinglie.

Your vearie friend,

R. Leycester."

We may well believe that the ardent fancy of young Sidney gazed with delight on the world of action, now first opening before him in Paris, the gay centre of the civilized world. His were the age and the spirit to yearn for action in its highest and noblest sense, and if unable yet to achieve, he rejoiced to witness and to learn. But, in order better to appreciate his interest in the shifting scenery of the time, we will endeavor to present a brief view of its most important features.

The twilight of the middle ages had been followed by the brightness of a new day, and Europe now trod with gigantic step the path of progress. The discovery of a new world of wonder and of wealth; the inventions of paper and of printing; the grand religious crisis of the Reformation; and the contemporaneous sovereignty of four of the greatest monarchs who ever graved their names upon the tablets of time, formed a combination of events such as will probably never again be witnessed by the tenants of our earth. The daring vitality of the new faith had assailed the bigotry of the old until it trembled with rage and fear. The portals of knowledge had responded to the talismanic *Sesame* of the press. The El Dorado of the West had filled from its exhaustless treasuries the coffers of the East, and had vastly extended commerce and navigation. Gustavus Vasa, the patriot King of Sweden, had delivered his country from the yoke of Denmark, and left upon its institutions the impress of his own liberal mind. Francis I., the warrior king of France, who even in defeat lost not his honour, had created in that country a golden age of letters. Charles V., whose conquests and whose schemes had dazzled Europe during his forty years of restless transit from Germany to Spain, and from Africa to the Italian States, had at last laid aside his sceptre for a scourge, and his imperial robe for a monastic gown. Solyman II. slept in a marble mausoleum in the city of Constantine and the Cæsars, where the cradle hymn of Christianity had long been replaced by the muezzin's call to prayer. The voice of the haughty Turk no longer woke the echoes of the Carpathian hills, or summoned to surrender the fortresses upon the Danube. The isles of Greece trembled not now beneath his destroying tread; and Venice, with new joy, flung her marriage ring into the waters of the Adriatic. Copernicus, Raphael, Michael

Angelo, Titian, Tasso, and Correggio, were the priests of science and the arts. All these, save two alone, had passed away; and with the abdication of Charles in 1556, and the death of Solyman ten years later, a new set of actors was marshalled on the stage. But that memorable era stands with pyramidal grandeur between the semi-barbarism of the mediæval and the enlightenment of modern times. It was a period when the human mind, after a long slumber in the toils of ignorance and prejudice, in which ideals of truth and knowledge had flitted before it in restless dreams, seemed suddenly waking to the songs of advancing Freedom. The thought of its own possible perfection seemed to mingle with its returning consciousness, and casting off each trace of lethargy, it rose, eager to meet and to vanquish all opposition to its progress and its triumph.

In the early summer of 1572, peace prevailed throughout all the important countries of Europe, although the fermentation of rancor and revenge heaved in silence beneath many a placid surface. England, under the administration of the last of the Tudors, breathed the free air of religious toleration. Cultivating her lands, and increasing her manufactures, multiplying her fleets, and enriching her exchequer, she already felt the fulfilment of the dying prophecy of her illustrious martyr at the fires of Oxford: "We shall this day kindle such a flame in England as will never be extinguished." The daughter of Henry VIII. and Anne Boleyn united to the coquettish vanity of her mother the imperious will of her father. Shrewd, subtle, and sagacious, not unvariable in love, but irreconcilable in hate, her character had doubtless been modified by her youthful sorrows when the prisoner of her jealous sister Mary; and perhaps by the influence of Edward VI. of whom she was the favourite sister; while her preceptor the good Archbishop Parker had inspired her mind with a zealous affection for the Church of which her father was the first legal defender.

Scotland, under the regency of the Earl of Murray, watched the sunset of her day of national sovereignty. Her beautiful and hapless Queen, the heroine of story and of song, was a prisoner at Fotheringay Castle, cherishing vain hopes of release, and planning desperate revenge upon the subjects whom she had never loved, and the rival cousin whom she had ever hated. Her fascinations of person and of manner had beguiled of homage every knightly man who ventured within the spell of her presence, and her romantic position as a woman and a Queen had unsheathed many a valiant sword in her behalf. But now, though she knew it not, fifteen dreary years of captivity were before her, ere her graceful form should bow beneath the headsman's axe. Though, like Joanna of Naples, the dark suspicion of a husband's murder brooded over her fame, (a suspicion which in both cases was deepened by immediate marriage with men accused of participation in the crime,) yet, like her, Mary is commended to merciful judgment by a plausible *perhaps.* Both were alike the victims of artful counsel from bad and designing men. Joanna's misfortunes were the retribution of her errors, but Mary's errors were the parasites of her misfortunes.

The vigorous administration of Ferdinand and Isabella, aided by the Cardinal Ximenes, (whose zeal and ability in the double duties of prelate and prime minister won the reverence of his country and the plaudits of the world,) together with the discovery of America and the conquest of Granada, gave to Spain, in the early part of the sixteenth century, a rank which she had never known before, and which she forfeited at its close. Her prosperity seemed a realization of some of those Oriental tales, in which, at the summons of the necromancer's wand an army of slaves bending beneath inestimable burdens comes forth from cave or mountain, or an argosy of perfumed treasures speeds over the sea. The gold and silver of Mexico and Peru freighted her ships. The commerce of the Jews, who were a large and well-established community, brought ever multiplying wealth to her cities. The last province of the Moors had surrendered to Spanish power, and the gates of the Alhambra reluctantly opened to the armies of the Cross. That gifted and romantic people combined the untamed grace of their native Arabia with a love of letters and of art that radiated its solitary light during eight centuries, while Europe sat in barbaric gloom. Painting and sculpture were forbidden by the Koran, but every ideal of poetic beauty was embodied in their architecture, and every known science was illustrated in their inventions and manufactures. We owe to them our arithmetical calculations, and the creation of paper; their silks excelled those of India, and their porcelain that of China, while the swords of Granada were famed throughout Europe. Their system of jurisprudence was a barrier against royal and aristocratic encroachment, and blessed them with an almost republican freedom. Nor should we fail to observe that, while almost the world beside had lost or neglected the lessons of Chaldean and Egyptian astronomy, and the stars seemed only night lamps in the vault above, the Moors still watched the heavens with philosophic interest, calculated the eclipses of the planets, established the obliquity of the ecliptic, divined the cause of the twilight, and solved the reason of the refraction of the atmosphere. The home of science was thus for long centuries amid these devotees of the faith of Islam.

Their history reminds us of the comment of Pyrrhus upon the Romans: "These barbarians are not so barbarous after all." When the avarice of Spain had absorbed their magnificent possessions, it would seem that policy alone should have dictated kindness to the vanquished; but here was enacted one of the most revolting scenes in the sad drama of "man's inhumanity to man." The Inquisition—that red right hand of hell—sent forth its demons to torture the disciples of Mahometanism into the love of Christ. True to a faith much loftier than such Christianity, they suffered death or exile rather than recant. The children of Abraham were victims of the same atrocious bigotry. It was estimated that in one year eight hundred thousand of this doomed nation were massacred or banished. As they controlled almost exclusively the commercial interests of the country, the retributive injury was great and lasting. After the death of the royal patrons of Columbus, and the accession of their grandson Charles V., Spain was agitated by a succession of civil disturbances arising from that monarch's preference for his German dominions, and from his ceaseless demands for pecuniary supplies. But notwithstanding these numerous exhausting influences, Philip II. found himself, on his father's abdication, master of the preponderating power in Europe. The Spanish fleet was the most formidable in the world save that of Turkey, and the Spanish was the language of fashion and of courtly parlance in Paris, in Vienna, in Turin, and in Milan.

From the death of Francis I. to the period of which we write, France was the theatre of religious tyranny and political faction. The weak administration of Charles IX., and the intrigues of his mother, Catherine de Medici, for personal dominion, fostered the spirits of violence and revolt. The houses of Guise and Montmorenci in the name of the Pope, and the princes of Condé in the name of the Reformation, fought for individual power rather than for religious principle. Every ambitious leader on either side collected an army of partisans; and, at one time, no less than fourteen of these marauding bands desolated the fair provinces watered by the Loire and the Garonne. The Protestants, infuriated by persecution, learned, like the Catholics, to be bitter in warfare and barbarous in triumph. The former pillaged Churches, and the latter burned Bibles. But Charles, alarmed by the ruinous condition of his finances, proclaimed an amnesty in 1570, promising to the Huguenots pardon for the past, and toleration for the future. The promise was as treacherous as the stealthy pause of a tiger before his fatal spring. The memory of Jarnac and Moncontour was only merged in new schemes of perfidy, silently matured in the dark counsels of the Italian Queen and the Duke of Guise.

"Time shall unlock what plaited cunning hides."

The Netherlands at this era presented a picture of intense dramatic interest. Though forming a portion of the inheritance of Philip II., they had never lovingly bent to the Spanish yoke, and after years of smothered passion, they were now ripe for rebellion. The cruelty and oppression of that haughty monarch, in his determined efforts to establish the Catholic worship, have no parallel in the pages of modern persecution. His fitting emissary, the Duke of Alva, preyed like a vulture upon the most industrious and wealthy cities in the world, typifying his merciless ferocity in his statue erected by himself in the market place at Antwerp, where he is represented as trampling on the necks of two smaller figures, emblematic of the States of the Netherlands. The same atrocious idea found utterance in his subsequent boast that in five years he had sent eighteen thousand heretics to the executioner. The peaceful inhabitants, whose only crime was their claim to liberty of conscience, and whose first trials began with the edict against it by Charles V. in 1550, flocked by thousands to England, Germany, and France, carrying with them arts and manufactures hitherto almost unknown in those countries, but henceforth a source to them of emolument and prosperity. Meanwhile, William of Orange, the silent hero of Holland's hope, wrought with patient zeal from his own mind, and life, and substance, the instruments of her release, unconsciously wreathing at the same time his patriot crown with the idolizing affection of her grateful sons and daughters. The signal gun of a long and most memor-

* Among many illustrations of a wealth which was certainly the product of industry, is a story of the wife of Philip the Fair of France, who, while making a tour with her royal spouse through Flanders, evidently expected to "create a sensation" among the Flemish dames by the splendor of her own attire. Looking with indignant surprise upon the glittering jewels and rich silks of the ladies of Bruges, she exclaimed, "I thought that I was the only Queen here, but I find six hundred Queens beside myself in this place."

able contest had just been fired. The sea-port town of Brille was seized from the Spanish guards by the Gueux or beggars, a combination of merchants and noblemen, whose wallet and staff, the symbols of their hatred and despair, now summoned to the rally, firm, true hearts, the denizens of humble hamlets, and of old feudal castles, boatmen from Zealand, and burghers from Antwerp, Amsterdam, and Leyden, until the canals, the rivers, and the sea-washed plains of the future battle-ground of Europe swarmed with heroes as desperate as those who defended the pass of Thermopylæ, swept through the English hosts at Bannockburn, or waved in triumph the banner of Switzerland and of Tell over the Austrian troops at Morgarten.

To the general reader, the history of no nation is more hopelessly chaotic than that of the German Empire and its dependencies, for three centuries preceding the reign of Charles V. Patience toils wearily through the confused details of wars between Dukes and Princes, wars for the elective imperial throne, wars for the sovereignty of Italy, contests against Popes, and battles against Infidels; Guelphs and Ghibelines now opposing hostile front to each other, and, anon, uniting their embattled squadrons against the common foe; one army swept away for the cross and another for the crescent; useless victories and ruinous defeats; now the Tiber bearing a crimson tribute to the sea, and again the plundered towns and wasted harvests of Austria, Hungary, and Germany, repeating the sad tale of desolation. The Reformation, too, through long years germinating in thoughtful minds, and born amid the convulsive throes of fanaticism and of faction, kindled new flames by its fervid purifying breath. But the elements were now hushed in happy silence. The reigning Emperor, Maximilian II., was too prudent and too pacific for the strife of either bigotry or dominion. A truce of twelve years with the Turks granted respite from his most dreaded foes, while the hymns of fraternal peace chimed through his extended principalities.

But while the jealous kinsmen of Christendom thus vibrated between friendship and hostility, there loomed before them a foreign enemy, whose giant footfall reverberated to the remotest corner of civilization. The Turkish name had ever been the synonym of indomitable will and merciless success, from the distant day when the military colonists that bore it emerged from the table lands of Tartary, until the resistless tide of their migration laved the ramparts of Venice and Vienna. We learn of their selling forbearance to China in exchange for splendid gifts; then of their alliance with Rome against the Persians; and their affluence of barbaric spoil appears in the story of the Khan Disabul, who received the ambassadors from the seven-hilled city in a tent festooned with silk, and decorated with a couch of pure and massive gold, supported on four golden peacocks, while cups, vases, and statues of gold and silver, were scattered profusely around. A few centuries later they swept away the pagodas of India, and overturned the caliphate at Bagdad; and having obtained by slow degrees the provinces of Asia Minor, they crossed the Hellespont, and poured their unfaltering armies over the Byzantine Empire. The degenerate Greeks were an easier prey than the stalwart bands of Hungary and Thrace. There was small glory in conquest over the superstitious people who destroyed their navy, because the protection of Deity was sufficient panoply against infidel might; and who confronted a phalanx of sabres with a daub of the Madonna. But the Turks met not everywhere such craven foes. Venice and the knights of Rhodes and of Malta wrote their own brilliant page in history. John Huniades, with his brave Hungarians, baffled them for many years, falling gloriously at last in the siege of Belgrade. The perverse pets of Turkish nurseries were terrified into obedience by his name, as were the Scottish children by that of the Black Douglas. Scanderbeg wrested from them by a daring stratagem his native Albania, and aided by his martial mountaineers, long defied that most redoubtable of Sultans, Mahomet II. Three thousand turbaned heads fell, it was said, by his single hand, and when the tidings of his death arrived, Mahomet, laying aside his Oriental immobility, actually danced for joy. Such was the prestige of this valorous patriot, that the Janizaries, forcing open his sepulchre, divided his bones into small fragments, and wore them encased in bracelets as amulets to inspire courage. The fall of Constantinople was delayed fifty years by the capture of Bajazet by Tamerlane, but its doom was written, said the Turks, in the pages of the Koran. The territory of the Cæsars was now reduced to the pitiful limit of sixteen miles. Monks and emperors, courtiers and clergy, insanely absorbed in political factions and religious polemics, drank the wines of Samos to the image of the Virgin, and helplessly waited for angelic aid. The Christian nations were busy with their civil wars, or indifferent to the fate of the last stronghold of the Greeks; and thus, when the Ottoman fleet triumphantly sailed up the

Bosphorus, and the troops of Mahomet unfurled the crescent before the gate of St. Romanus only four Genoese ships came to the rescue of the besieged. Two hundred and fifty thousand Turks swept the city with the weapons of both ancient and modern warfare—gunpowder, battering rams, and liquid fire; and after forty days the Hippodrome, and the church of St. Sophia, the treasures of Roman, of Grecian, and of Egyptian art, and the wealth of the Byzantine libraries passed into Saracen hands. Unlike Boniface VIII., who, with the tiara on his head, and the keys and the cross in either hand, had "lived a Pope and would die a Pope," the last of a hundred emperors, nobler in death than in life, flinging from him the imperial mantle, died with heroic dignity among the common soldiers, and was distinguished in the heaps of slain only by the golden eagles on his shoes.

Still fulfilling their predestined career, the Turks, in the sixteenth century, were the objects of universal respect and fear. Solyman II. dictated to the several monarchs of Europe, in terms which though very serious then, now provoke a smile. The Emperor of Germany he called simply *Charles*, because, said he, "there cannot exist two emperors on the face of the earth; there is only one, namely, the Sultan, just as there is only one God." Said the grand vizier Ibrahim to the ambassadors from Germany, "How can Charles dare to entitle himself King of Jerusalem? Does he not know that the Grand Signior is master at Jerusalem? I know that Christian nobles visit Jerusalem in the garb of beggars: does Charles believe that if he were to make the same pilgrimage he would on that account be King of Jerusalem? I will for the future issue orders forbidding any Christian to enter the place."

To Ferdinand of Austria proposing to petition the Sultan for a part of Hungary, the patronizing Ibrahim dictated an appeal in the following terms: "King Ferdinand, thy son, considers all he possesses as thy property, and every thing in his hands as belonging to thee. He was not aware that thou wished'st to keep Hungary to thyself; for, had he known it, he never would have waged war there. But since thou, oh father! desirest to have that country, he offers thee his best wishes for thy health and prosperity!" The effect of this enforced humility is shown in a letter of Busbeck, the Austrian ambassador: "When I compare the power of the Turks with our own, the consideration fills me with anxiety and dismay, and a strong conviction forces itself on my mind that we cannot long resist the destruction that awaits us. They possess immense wealth, strength unbroken, a perfect knowledge of the art of war, patience under every difficulty, union, order, frugality, and a constant state of preparation. On our side, exhausted finances, universal luxury, our national spirit broken by repeated defeats, mutinous soldiers, mercenary officers, intemperance, and a total neglect or contempt of military discipline fill up the dismal catalogue." *

* As the centuries file slowly on, it is impressive to note how the battlements of pride and the bulwarks of power tremble and fall at their approach.

In 1844 Lord Aberdeen writes to the English minister at Constantinople, in allusion to the execution of Christians for their religion; "Your Excellency will therefore press upon the Turkish government, that if the Porte has any regard for the friendship of England, if it has any hope that in the hour of peril or adversity, that protection which has more than once saved it from destruction will be extended to it, it must renounce absolutely, and without equivocation, the barbarous custom which has called forth this remonstrance."

The giant has survived his appointed time, and his decrepid existence now hangs upon the fiat of the younger nations who once paled before his menace, and sued for his benign regard.

CHAPTER III.

WITH those genial readers who can fill even a feeble outline with vivid form and color, interblending their own cultured thought and fancy with the imperfect tracery of the written page, let us hope to call forth from the misty past the glittering throng that held high holiday in Paris, in that far distant summer when Philip Sidney, having forsaken, as we have seen, the classic calm of the English University, now studied a new phase of life. Presented by Sir Francis Walsingham to the French king, his ingenuous dignity of mien attracted the fancy of Charles IX., who testified his regard by appointing him to the office of gentleman of his bedchamber.

The disparity of age between these two young men was four years, but there can be found no stronger contrast than that which existed between their characters. The scion of Valois united strange mental and moral contradictions. At twelve years he threw off the regency, declaring that he "would no longer be kept in a box like the old jewels of the crown." At twenty-two he loved letters, and generously patronized literary men, delighted in the mechanical arts, and often wrought iron at the forge. Music was his passion, and he abstained from fruits and swallowed emetics for the improvement of his voice—an expedient more innocent than his favorite diversion of killing animals, to watch their dying agonies. The code of Machiavel was his sacred manual, and the motto of his grandfather Louis XI.—"He who knows not how to dissemble knows not how to reign"—was his boasted watchword. The offspring of a weak father and a profligate mother, born to power, and tutored to its abuse, perverted by false theories, blinded by evil examples, desecrating his talents to vice, and his tastes to brutality, the most lenient look of posterity upon this modern Nero is one of pity and disgust.

"Whether your time call you to live or die, do both like a prince," wrote Sidney a few years later. "As the sun disdains not to give light to the smallest worm, so a virtuous prince protects

* "A judicious prince will from time to time commit acts of wanton cruelty that his subjects may appreciate how much they are indebted to him for not being constantly wanton and cruel."—*Machiavel.*

the life of his meanest subject." "And as he is most wise to see what is best, he is most just in performing what he sees." "Such a prince especially measures his greatness by his goodness; and if for any thing he love greatness, it is because therein he may exercise his goodness. He makes his life the example of his laws, and his laws, as it were, his axioms arising out of his deeds."

We have no record of Sidney's impressions of his royal patron, unless we accept these sentiments as an inverted portrait. We readily infer from them that his pure mind suffered no distortion from the flatteries of royal favor, or the subtleties of courtly art.

It was the 22d of August, and all Paris glittered with pageantry and pomp, and rang with festal glee. In the Church of St. Germain was solemnized the marriage of King Henry of Navarre, afterwards Henry IV. of France, with Marguerite of Valois, sister of Charles IX. The bridegroom was handsome, good, and predestined to the bravery that long after made his white plume a rallying point on the field of Ivry; for he entered the world to the stirring music of a martial band, his first draught of life was a sip of wine, and with naked feet and bare head he sported in childhood with the hardy little peasantry of his native hills. But, for some unknown reason, the fair bride yielded no willing troth. When led to the altar, and asked by the priest if she consented to the marriage, instead of her expected response, an ominous silence ensued. The question was repeated, and Charles took care to secure her seeming assent, through the ludicrous little stratagem of forcing her head forward by striking the back of her neck. No sentimental union of hearts and hands was this, but the forced result of profound political craft. On this pivot was to turn the fate of Protestantism in France. That country had long been, as we have seen, the battle-ground of religious faction. The Catholics, led by the powerful families of Guise and Montmorenci, and the Protestants under Coligni, the Condés, and the princes of Navarre, vibrated between sanguinary feud and hollow truce. Fostered by the persecution of the two preceding reigns, the faith of the Reformers had spread rapidly through the provinces, and many men of high rank and talent defiantly exchanged the worship of the Host for the study of the Bible. Sincere in devotion, pure in purpose, loyal as citizens and as subjects, the Huguenots asked only liberty of conscience and the privilege of prayer. But, at length, stung by insult, and exasperated by injury, the spirit of religion was merged in the spirit of resistance, and they were forced to the belligerent attitude of a hostile army. Philip II. and the Pope had long looked with malignant alarm upon their rapid increase in numbers and strength; aided, as they sometimes were, by troops and supplies from the Queen of England, and encouraged by the ever manifest sympathy of her subjects. The spirit of reform seemed to rise from every conflict with loftier and more stately crest. It regarded the howls of the Vatican as those of a decrepit lion in his den. The wily bigot of Spain was a more potent foe. Allied by marriage with the royal family of Valois, of the same faith, and the same unscrupulous perfidy, his inexorable designs upon the heretics of the Netherlands obviously reflected upon the heretics of France. Seven years before, the Duke of Alva and Queen Isabella met, in private conference at Bayonne, Catherine de Medici and Charles IX. The Duke, always equal to enterprises of colossal crime, was empowered by his royal master to concoct a scheme for the simultaneous massacre of the Protestants, throughout France and the Low Countries. The plan was, this time, a failure. The Queen Mother, true to her favorite maxim —"divide in order to govern"—preferred to employ her Medicean arts on the alternate factions, as might best serve her own purpose of dominion. To preserve the balance of power by curbing the ascendant interest, she lent her influence sometimes to a Condé, sometimes to a Guise. But the Spanish leaven worked, and the crude thought swelled to consistent shape. In 1570, Charles proclaimed a general amnesty. The most specious promises of pardon, and of the free exercise of their religion, were extended to the Huguenots. The King said that the august marriage was intended as an additional assurance of his sincerity and good-will towards his heretic people, to ratify the peace now of two years duration. All the noted Protestants in the realm, from the ancient and proud noblesse to those of recent rank and reputation, were invited to Paris to witness the ceremony which should absorb forever all party animosities. Lulled into security by these plausible professions, they now thronged the gay city in vast and joyous companies, and fearlessly mingled in its nuptial revelries. Fêtes, dances, and masked balls filled with Circean draughts the intoxicated nights; tournaments and other equestrian sports chased the fleeting days. The Louvre offered its fascinations to the veteran soldiers of hard-fought battles; youthful cavaliers won new conquests among the flirting beauties, who, adorned with huge fardingales, tortuous stays, and Spanish cosmetics, came in highborn dignity something short of the English ladies of the same period. Here stood a stately group of Huguenot lords, talking in low tones of the recent defeat at Mons of brave Count Louis of Nassau, and mourning that the aid kindly sent by their king had failed against Spanish guile. And there were men of letters clustered around Ronsard and Montaigne; and here, again, was the English minister Walsingham, placid and composed as ever, but mentally striving to divine what new intrigue could be hidden beneath this fantastic show. The Lords Burleigh and Leicester had been invited by the King, but fortunately stayed away, for it was shrewdly guessed afterward, that two so powerful Protestants had been better off across the Channel than in the treacherous atmosphere of Paris.

Sidney looked with charmed eye upon this rare assemblage of princely personages, most of whom, though but few years older than himself, had already achieved distinction in either camp or court. Men, in that day, entered early on the duties of active life. Assassination, war, and unskilful medical science, swept rapidly through the ranks of manhood, and youth was summoned to the vacancy. Sir Henry Sidney, as his son remembered, had been sent on a mission to

France, at the age of twenty-one. First in this brilliant throng, was Henry of Navarre, with his suite of eight hundred gentlemen.

> "Oh was there ever such a knight, in friendship or in war,
> As our Sovereign Lord, King Henry, the soldier of Navarre."

The magnetism which attracts two kindred natures, revealing to each the mental harmony unobserved by others, drew silently its mysterious cords around the youthful Sidney and the gallant prince. A true friendship, merging in its sweet solvent all exterior distinctions, was formed between them, and perpetuated through life.

> "See, thro' plots and counterplots—
> Thro' gain and loss—thro' glory and disgrace—
> Along the plains where passionate Discord rears
> Eternal Babel—still the holy stream
> Of human happiness glides on!"

Sidney doubtless met the Admiral Coligni, the stanch old champion of the faith he loved, and the indomitable leader of its armies, long honored with high trust, but preserving through his integrity and hospitality the narrow limit of his ancestral acres. The thoughtful Prince of Condé, cousin of Navarre, was another Huguenot of note; Montgomery, too, who perhaps felt little pleasure in the revels of the court, since his fatal lance had pierced the golden visor of Henry II., in a tournament, twelve years before. In Mornay Du Plessis, who, though only twenty-three years old, was already distinguished for his learning, his sagacity, and his bold defence of Protestantism, Sidney found another friend. These grave men, and others there, eyed with distrust the ostentatious gayeties thus forced upon them, and sometimes thought, perhaps, that Catholic faith to heretics might resemble that of the Milanese to Frederick Barbarossa,—"Remember, if you have our oath, we have not sworn to keep it."

Conspicuous on the other side were the military stars,—De Retz, De Ferrière, and the Marshal Tavannes, whose heroic feats at the battle of Renti so delighted Francis I., that, rushing through the heat and smoke of the engagement, he tore from his own neck the order of St. Michael, and threw it around that of his brave general. Yet more prominent was the Duke of Anjou, the hero of Jarnac and Moncontour, and recently, at the instance of his ambitious mother, a suitor of Queen Elizabeth—a reluctant suitor, too, for her midsummer charms seemed to his nineteen springs a distasteful incumbrance upon the crown of England. But preëminent among them all, was the stately and handsome Duke of Guise, one of the most keen and daring spirits of the day, having numbered only twenty-two years, but already renowned for his skilful defence of Poictiers, and a perfect representative of his bold, turbulent, and ambitious family.* The keystone of this

* Several stories are told of this Duke of Guise, illustrative of his imperious will and unfaltering decision of character. He had married a princess of Cleves, equally remarkable for her beauty and her levity. The patience of the Duke and the faith of the public having been considerably transcended in the very *empressé* regard between herself and a young man named St. Maigrin, she was requested by her husband to decline attending a ball and supper given by the Queen-Mother, in which the ladies of the court were to be served by their favourite cavaliers, dressed in the livery of their mistresses. The Duke reasonably suggested that additional scandal might arise from the presence of the Duchess under the escort of St. Maigrin, and earnestly desired her to remain at home. The obstinate beauty—much like those of a later day—persisted in going to the ball, and did not return until six o'clock in the morning. She had just sought repose in bed, when the door very slowly opened, and her irate lord deliberately walked in, followed by an aged servant, bearing a bowl of broth. Locking the door, he solemnly advanced to the bedside, and addressed her in portentous tones: "Madame, although you refused last night to do what I desired, you shall do it now. Your dancing must have heated you a little, and I insist upon your instantly drinking this broth that I have prepared for you." The Duchess burst into tears, and feeling that the poisoned chalice, as she supposed it to be, was inevitable, begged the privilege of seeing her confessor. This was refused by the Duke, who having compelled her to

social arch was Catherine de Medici. The craft of her country, the pride of her family, her own thirst for power, her reckless will, her placid dissimulation, were painted in her fine, well-pro-

swallow the draught, left the room, again locking the door. After four hours he returned. "I fear," said he, in a softened tone, "that you have passed these hours unpleasantly. I also fear that I have been the cause. Judge then of all the hours that you have made me spend as unpleasantly as these. Be comforted, however. You have nothing to fear. I am willing in my turn to believe that I have nothing to apprehend. But for the future, if you please, we will avoid playing these little tricks upon each other."

The Duke was once setting out on a dangerous expedition, when his brother, the Duke of Mayenne, urged him to deliberate. "Brother," replied he, "be assured that what I could not resolve upon in a quarter of an hour I could never resolve upon, though I were to spend my whole life in the effort."

Dancing one night at the Louvre, a lady said to him, in a low tone, "It is really very fine for you to be amusing yourself here, when your enemies are taking from you the town of Meaux." Startled by the news, he yet preserved his self-possession, and having learned all he could from his fair informant, who was in the secrets of the opposite party, he ordered one of his officers in waiting to have ready for him, at the Hotel de Guise, a fleet Arabian horse. Dancing until the ball was over, he then went home, and to bed, quietly dismissing his attendants. As soon as they had left him, he rose, and mounting his steed, rode to Meaux, a distance of thirty miles. He found the city in confusion, and his partisans in prison, but hastily collecting his soldiers, he released the prisoners, nounced features, and spoke in every movement of her queenly form. Uniting, like her son, odd contrasts of taste and employment, she was a liberal patroness of literature and the arts, excelled in conversation, and was equally devoted to embroidery and intrigue. France had been happier if the Queen Regent had contented herself with plots in silk and conspiracies in tapestry, and the device on the ship that landed her at Marseilles as the bride of Henry II. (representing the sun, with the motto underneath, "I bring light, and fine weather,") had been a less bitter jest. She possessed the restless, vindictive cruelty, without the courage, of Brunehaut of Austrasia, but her master passion was the love of dominion. Her ascendency over the young king was as absolute as that of Blanche of Castile over St. Louis; not that Charles gave to her either affection or esteem, but that, to a mind at once unreasoning, timid, fitful, and impatient, concession was easier than

and harangued the citizens in the market place with so happy a mingling of command and persuasion that, like Richard II. in Wat Tyler's insurrection, he swayed the rebels to his absolute control.

His abilities and popularity afterwards excited the jealousy of Henry III., who ordered his assassination, and exclaimed, as he saw his majestic form rigid in death, "Mon Dieu, comme il est grand, étant mort!"

resistance. "I know not whom to trust," said the hapless sovereign, "my secretaries of state are not faithful to me; the Comte de Retz is a Spaniard; my brother Anjou is full of Italian deceit; my mother, of turbulent self-will." He might have learned the negative lesson—whom not to trust—from Philip Sidney, whose keen observation gathered from these motley scenes many a note for future thought. "Take heed," said he, "how you place your confidence upon any other ground than proof of virtue. Neither length of acquaintance, mutual secrecy, nor height of benefits, can bind a vicious heart; no man being good to others that is not good in himself."

When Pius V. sent his legate to remonstrate with the French king on the marriage of his sister with a heretic, the latter taking from his finger a diamond ring, and giving it to the messenger, replied, "I wish that I could explain my purpose now; but his Holiness will one day be the first to praise my piety and zeal." Younger in treachery than his mother and her confederates, Charles had regarded with horror the proposed massacre of St. Bartholomew.

> "The colour of the king did come and go
> Between his purpose and his conscience."

Maddened by taunt, and overpowered by entreaty, the latent demon at last came forth. "I consent," he cried, "but let not a single Huguenot remain alive, to reproach me with the deed."

In due time, all the Catholics in Paris were in the secret, and never was secret better kept. It seems strange that no friend or kinsman should have relented at last, to save the innocent and the dear; but no cruelty is so remorseless as the cruelty of the bigot. The provost of Paris, and his principal officers, were at first obstinate in resistance to the scheme, but were soon awed by the threats of Tavannes. The sky was not all sunny to the doomed Protestants. Clouds of gloom and distrust hung darkly in the distance, visible to prescient eyes, and heralded by warning voices. Against counsel, menace, and entreaty, the King of Navarre sought his promised bride: remonstrances and prayers followed Coligni to the very gates of Paris. As the latter bade adieu to his wife at Chatillon, one of his faithful peasants fell at his feet,—"Oh good master, why will you throw yourself away? I shall never see you again! You will die, and all who go with you." A captain of Langorain, who accompanied him thither, took his leave in a few days with the ominous suggestion, "There is too much caressing here. I had rather be safe with fools, than perish with those who think themselves wise." Although to these prophetic surmises was added the startling suspicion that the recent death of Jeanne of Navarre, mother of the king, resulted from the poisoned odor of a pair of gloves bought from René, the perfumer of Catherine de Medici, and the fact of an attempt upon Coligni's own life, by a pistol fired into his carriage,—yet the good Admiral was entirely assured by the flatteries of Charles. "He could not believe in perfidy at twenty-two," says Martin; "it seemed to him that the virtues implanted by nature had gradually vanquished the evils of education, and that the blood of a noble warrior race spoke more loudly than the lessons of Birague and Des Gondi." Meanwhile, this scion of "a noble warrior race" rehearsed the anticipated excitement of St. Bartholomew in a daily massacre of rabbits, and each night he met in secret conclave the master tragedians of the infernal drama thus contemptibly typified. Anjou, Angoulême, the Duke of Guise, and the Queen Mother, with her four intimate counsellors—De Retz, Tavannes, De Nevers, and Birague—stole from midnight mirth to midnight murder;—one hour figuring in the mask of folly and the next in that of crime; and, as hilarious voices rang through echoing corridors and gorgeous salons, deep bitter tones in an upper chamber breathed the doom of the revellers below.

The fatal hour approached. It was Sunday eve, and just six days after the royal marriage. The Catholic citizens, marked by a white scarf upon the left arm and a white cross upon the hat, were assembled at midnight at the Hotel de Ville. Twelve hundred arquebusiers were distributed along the Seine, through the streets and in the Huguenot quarter. The Duke of Guise, frenzied with the memory of his father's fate, with hatred for his natural enemies, the heretics, and with ambition as the great Catholic leader, commanded the deadly brigade.

The king retired to his room attended by several Protestant lords. He could not stifle a reluctant pang as he looked upon these brave and genial companions, and especially Rochefoucault, with whom he often laughed and jested until night waned into morning. He would have persuaded him to remain in the safety of the royal chamber. But Rochefoucault, little dreaming the penalty of refusal, declined the invitation, and, with edifying piety, the King exclaimed as he departed, "I see God wills that he should perish!" In the chamber of Catherine de Medici, as the Queen of Navarre offered the good-night kiss to her sister, the Duchess of Lorraine, the latter burst into tears, and passionately exclaimed, "My sister, do not go!" The Queen Mother frowned, and calling the Duchess aside, forbade her to detain her sister. "You will sacrifice her," cried the Duchess; "if any thing is discovered, they will take revenge on her." "*Whatever happens*," was the answer, "she must go, lest her stay excite suspicion." Thus were the sweet charities of love sacrificed on the altar of hate.

The fearful parts had all been assigned. The players waited, in mute suspense, the signal stroke of the great clock of St. Germain l'Auxerrois. The secret council were assembled for the last time; the plot was finished; and, with suppressed tones and furtive glances, they too listened for the knell of death. The city lay hushed in that oppressive stillness which precedes a hurricane—the victims, in unsuspecting sleep, the executioners, on stealthy guard. Suddenly one deep vibration of the ponderous bell broke upon the silent air, followed by the sharp sound of a pistol. The lingering spark of humanity in the wretched king now flickered in expiring light.

> "He started, like a guilty thing,
> Upon a fearful summons."

In trembling repentance, he sped a messenger to the Hotel de Guise, to recall the mandate. It was too late. Already the fiery Duke paced the court below Coligni's window, impatient for the tidings of his death. "It is God that calls us," said the good Admiral to his terrified attendants, as the clash of arms and the fierce shouts of men broke upon their slumbers; "I have long been ready to die; save yourselves, if possible." "Besme!" cried Guise to the German assassin, "have you finished? Then throw him from the window that we may see for ourselves." "Courage, friends," shouted Angoulême, as he spurned the mangled body with his foot; "we have begun well, let us also finish well." Thus fell one of the best and bravest heroes of the age. Eminent, like Martinuzzi of Hungary, as a patriot and a soldier, he met a similar death with equal intrepidity.

The Comte de Rochefoucault was roused by a heavy knock upon his door; and, six masked men entering, he fancied that the King, in frolic mood, was visiting him in disguise. His merry question was answered by a dagger buried in his heart. Teligni, son-in-law of the Admiral, brave and universally beloved, sought refuge on a roof. He was pursued by some of the courtiers, but they had not the courage to take a life so dear, and the deed was left for the guards of Anjou.

And now through the quivering air rang the tumult of the hosts of hell—the discharge of fire-arms, the clang of bells, the shouts of the pursuers, the shrieks of the flying, the piteous cries of the wounded and the dying. Mangled bodies fell heavily from the windows; dissevered limbs strewed the streets; crimson streams hurried to the crimson river. No innocence, no age found mercy. The dead soldier floated down the Seine, side by side with the cradle of the living infant. Even childhood caught the mania of murder. The boy of ten years old strangled the infant of as many months. Nor were the white cross and the scarf a sure protection. Family feuds, the rivalries of love, the jealousies of place, now found quick redress among the Catholic ranks. Sons shot the fathers who had lived too long; heirs claimed by the sword their tardy inheritance; the discharge of a pistol would liquidate a debt; the stroke of a poniard would settle a disputed suit. Carts rumbling over the stones, freighted with the dying and the dead, encountered carts laden with their pillaged spoils. From the windows of the Louvre, Charles IX. continually howled, "Kill! kill!" while Catherine and her maids of honor laughed with ribald jest over the corpses of the gallant men with whom they had danced and feasted a few hours before. Woman's tenderness and man's humanity were alike palsied in these orgies of the fiends. Science furnished no shield; art, no exemption. Goujon, the "Correggio of sculpture," was slain with the chisel in his hand, and his eye intent upon the half-carved statue. Ramus, the learned philosopher who first dared to repudiate the doctrines of Aristotle, was found in his hidden retreat by his rival Charpentier. Ramus offered all his fortune as the price of his life The ransom was accepted, but the bond was sealed with death. "Bleed! bleed!" shouted Tavannes; "bleeding is as good in August as in May!" Navarre and the Prince of Condé were spared only by a superstition of the Queen Mother. A friendly astrologer had predicted that they would in future be loyal and pacific, and the prophecy saved their lives. But though exempted from the general carnage, they were compelled to abjure their faith. "Death, Mass, or the Bastile!" cried the King, as they were brought before him. The young Baron de Rosni, afterwards the illustrious Sully, was saved by flying to the college of Bourgogne, with a Catholic book under his arm. Montgomery escaped, in night apparel, through one of the city gates, and rode without pause a hundred miles, until he reached his own chateau. Several illustrious lives were saved by a similar flight, and hundreds of Huguenots found refuge in the hospitable homes of England.*

Seven days the unheeded sun glared on the carnival of terror, and seven nights the stars looked

* Merlin, the chaplain of Coligni, concealed himself in a hay-loft; and it was recorded in the next synod that he subsisted for some time on eggs, daily laid by a hen which had made its nest near his place of safety.

Martin brightens these dark annals by a story of generous greatness, which carries us back, as he says, to "the heroes of Scandinavia," or reminds us perhaps of the kingly conduct of Edward III. to Eustace de Ribaumont, or that of the Black Prince at Poictiers. Two gentlemen of different faith, and from distant provinces, now chanced to meet in Paris. A deadly feud had long existed between them, which they had often sought occasion to settle by single combat. Regnier, who was a Protestant, felt that his death was inevitable, when Vezins suddenly entered his apartment with a drawn sword in his hand, accompanied by several armed men. Falling on his knees, Regnier offered the last prayer of the dying. "Rise, and follow me," cried his foe, conducting him to a spot where stood two horses, and a company of mounted attendants. Regnier, ignorant of the fate awaiting him, was led in profound silence, during a ride of several days, to the gates of his own chateau. "I present you," said Vezins, "with your steed, and with your life; but do not therefore imagine that I ask your friendship. You still are free to be friend or foe."

down upon the ghastly dead. The royal orders had extended through France, and with few exceptions they were obeyed. Not less than fifty thousand souls in the provinces, and ten thousand in the city of Paris, bore to distant spheres their fearful witness of the tragedy of St. Bartholomew. The tidings flew to every palace, remote and near, and while Protestant Europe was paralyzed with horror, Spain expressed her exultation; the plaudits of the Pope were sent with jubilant haste to the French king, and paintings, poems, and medals, commemorative of the pious deed, were added to the treasures of the Vatican. Maximilian II., though the father-in-law of Charles, openly declared his indignation; and the Court of England treated Fenelon, the French ambassador, with marked resentment. Though long a favourite with the ladies and courtiers, they received him in deep mourning, with countenances of reproachful gloom, and deigned neither look nor word as he passed through the rooms leading to the presence-chamber. Thousands of brave Englishmen burned with impatience to hasten to the relief of the intrepid Huguenots, who had now ensconced themselves in the stronghold of Rochelle. But the wary Elizabeth, true to her usual impassive policy, and conscious of her perilous position, as a solitary Protestant sovereign against the perfidious trio of Rome, France, and Spain, quieted her conscience by a few grave animadversions upon the perjury of Charles, and calmed her subjects by the promise of secret aid to their despairing brethren.

CHAPTER IV.

THE signal-bell of St. Germain was Philip Sidney's first warning of the unparalleled *coup d'etat* that wakened France upon that "awful morn." The penetrative art of the wily English minister had, for once, been baffled by Medicean craft, and thus his countrymen were all unconscious of the sleeping volcano on which they trod in fearless and festive measure. His house was their immediate refuge, and there Sidney remained until, the personal danger being past, he could pursue his intended travels. Walsingham, who seemed to be much impressed with what he termed, in a letter to Lord Leicester, the rare gifts of his nephew, made every provision for the safety of the wanderer, and secured for him through Lorrain, the companionship of the good Dean of Winchester. Perhaps a prophetic instinct may have warmed the heart of Sir Francis, and dimly revealed in the distance a closer link between himself and his youthful guest. For even on this blood-stained soil, were sown the seeds of life and love ; and here Sidney first saw, we are told, his future wife, the Lady Frances Walsingham, then a beautiful child, whose passionate grief for the Huguenots called forth his sympathizing and tender regard.

From the brief records of our hero's progress, we learn of his passing through Strasburg and Heidelberg to Frankfort; pausing, we may believe, in the former city, at least long enough to bestow a tribute of admiration upon the celebrated cathedral, with its elaborate and delicately wrought tower, its famous clock, and its vast window of richly painted glass, then recently completed. In Heidelberg too, that picturesque old town, nestling in the vine-clad valley of the Neckar, then flourishing with commerce and uninjured by the bombardments and assaults of later years, we may fancy his visits to the ancient castle, the residence of the Electors Palatine, interesting both from its varied fortunes and its architectural grandeur; thence to the Church of St. Peter, to whose door Jerome of Prague attached his theses, and expounded them to the crowd in the churchyard adjoining; and again we may see him in the venerable University, one of the oldest in Germany, gazing with a student's awe upon the valuable books and manuscripts, which, in the scarcity of straw, were afterwards ignobly used in the thirty years war, to litter the cavalry of the conqueror Tilly.

Sidney's stay in Frankfort was of several months duration. He resided with Andrew Wechel, a noted printer of that day, and also a man of learning, for in the sixteenth century printers were scholars too, and their houses were the favorite resorts of men of taste and letters. Here Sidney formed an acquaintance with Hubert Languet, an estimable and accomplished French gentleman, lately a professor of civil law in the University of Padua, a friend of Melancthon, and an honored confidant of Gustavus of Sweden, and of William of Orange. His graceful urbanity of manner, extraordinary conversational gifts, marvellous erudition, extended political knowledge, and unpretending goodness, rendered him one of the brightest ornaments of the times. To him Sidney was indebted for much instruction in the governments, laws, and usages of nations, by which he was fitted for the duties of a diplomatist and statesman; and with unwearied heart and watchful eye this kind Mentor sought in his two years' abode upon the continent, to guard him from evil and temptation, to fortify and exalt his native virtues, and to guide his aspiring mind. It was high praise to win the warm and lasting friendship of this distinguished man, who, first attracted by Sidney's countenance and discourse, afterwards said of him, "That day on which I first beheld him with my eyes, shone propitious to me." He is thus gratefully celebrated by Sir Philip in the Arcadia:

"The song I sang old Languet had me taught,
Languet, the shepherd best swift Ister knew,
For clarkly read, and hating what is naught,
For faithful heart, clean hands, and mouth as true,
With his sweet skill my soulless youth he drew
To have a feeling taste of Him that sits
Beyond the heaven, far more beyond your wit.

. . . .

His good strong staff my slippery youth upbore;
He still hoped well, because I lovèd truth."

The letters of Languet to Sir Philip, written in Latin, have been much commended for their admirable sentiments and classic elegance of style. Unfortunately, but a small portion of Sidney's share in the correspondence has been preserved. The table-talk at the house of Andrew Wechel would be to us a pleasant record, but we are left to fancy the sparkling conversations of the erudite printer and his guests; how they talked of the mystical Platonism and the Aristotelian logic which divided the philosophy of Europe, yet untouched by the Promethean fire of Bacon and Des Cartes; of the struggling hopes of their revered religion, in these tempestuous times; of Italian literature, still irradiating Christendom with the glory, which, reflected from the two preceding centuries, was not yet sensibly obscured by the meretricious taste and the political despotism that were beginning to shed their baneful influence upon the present era; of Venetian splendor, of Roman art, and of a thousand other themes that kindled the enthusiasm of the ardent Sidney. With reluctant adieus, he at last severed himself from the delightful society at Frankfort, and, laden with rich memories and garnered lore proceeded to Vienna, in September, 1573.

The capital of the Germanic Empire could not then boast the attractive features that have since rendered it one of the most brilliant cities of Europe. But the famous Church of St. Stephen, and some other types of that stately and gorgeous architecture whose creation ceased with the age of Christian idolatry that inspired it; the University and the imperial Library, the most distinguished in Germany save that of Heidelberg, were objects of interest to our traveller; as also were, both here and in the other cities of his sojourn, the works of the old German painters, so remarkable for their microscopic exactness and minute elaboration, of Von Eyck, who revolutionized his art by the introduction of oils, of Kranach, of Holbein, and of Albert Durer, the Raphael of his country, and the inventor of engravings upon copper.

Sidney here applied himself with especial zeal to the study of those accomplishments which were deemed essential to the finish of a high-born cavalier; fencing, the use of arms in tournament and tilt, tennis playing, music, and, above all, horsemanship. His preceptor in the latter art was the chief equerry in the Emperor's stables, to whose eloquent partiality for his profession Sidney thus alludes in his Defence of Poesy.

"When the right vertuous E. W.* and I were at the Emperor's court together, we gave ourselves to learn horsemanship of John Pietro Pugliano, one that with great commendation held the place of Esquire in his Stable; and he, according to the fertileness of the Italian wit, did not only afford us the demonstration of his practice, but sought to enrich our minds with the contemplation therein, which he thought most precious. But with none I remember mine eares were at any time more loaden, than when

* Edward Wotton, the brother of Sir Henry Wotton.

(either angered with slow payment, or moved with our learner-like admiration) hee exercised his speech in the praise of his faculty. He said souldiers were the noblest estate of mankind, and horsemen the noblest of souldiers. He said they were the masters of war, and ornaments of peace, speedy goers and strong abiders, triumphers both in camps and courts; nay, to so unbeleeved a point, he proceeded, as that no earthly thing bred such wonder to a Prince, as to be a good horseman. Then would he adde certaine praises, by telling what a peerless beast the horse was, the only serviceable Courtier without flattery, the beast of most beauty, faithfulnesse, courage, and such more, that if I had not bin a peece of a logician before I came to him, I think he would have perswaded me to have wished myself a horse."

To Venice, the brilliant centre of taste and fashion, and still the proud claimant of a maritime sovereignty that was rapidly passing into other hands, Philip Sidney next directed his way. What motley pictures of the past and present must have flitted before his eye as he stood upon the Rialto, or trod the tesselated pavement of St. Mark,—from the far-off day when the fugitive fishermen of these sterile isles sold their humble wares upon the neighboring coasts, on, through centuries of industry and toil, until the flag of the fearless republic floated defiantly over every sea, and commanded respect from every people. He looked back upon the dreary ages when darkness brooded over Europe, and Art had taken refuge in the city of Constantine, and saw in Venice the only causeway through which the gorgeous trappings and luxurious commodities of the East were conveyed to Germany and France. He saw the mountains of Istria furnishing flocks for the woollen fabrics of this busy people; the coast of Frioul, mulberry trees for their silks; the islands of the Levant, their sugar-canes and wines; their ships and their treasures more than once gladly borrowed by kings and nobles, during the wars in Palestine; and workmen from Athens, Thebes, and Corinth, finding rich reward in the reproduction of their classic models of sculpture, while antique gems, mosaics and bronzes, the marble of Palladio and the canvas of Titian, now enriched their churches and their palaces. Unaffected alike by Oriental voluptuousness and by Gothic barbarism, their prosperity and their refinement kept equal pace; while the jealous, relentless despotism of their government repressed domestic treason and precluded foreign guile.

But the tide had even now turned, and was

sweeping away from the mistress of the seas the golden treasures of her youth.

The discovery of America, and of a new passage to the Indies by the Cape of Good Hope diverting from the Adriatic the merchandise of Asia, the jealousy of Spain, the commercial rivalry of other nations, the inroads of the Turks, and the loss of Cyprus and Candia, were the causes of a decline which neither enterprise could arrest, nor vigilance avert.

In 1574, Venice was the neutral ground on which men of all creeds and countries could meet safely, and with pleasure; it was still the emporium of trade, and the rendezvous of poets, painters, and sculptors. Flitting about its canals, were young cavaliers from England and France, bartering for the silks and laces indispensable to their attire, or for the polished weapons and gilded leather equally essential to their equestrian display. Turbaned Turks, now on an embassy from Constantinople, commanded respectful notice in the halls of audience; for the Doge and the Council of Ten feared nothing so much as these insatiable foes. Military men from Stockholm and Madrid exchanged admiration over the magnificent arsenal from whose ramparts the gigantic granite lions of the Piræus, trophies of Venetian conquest in Athens, looked down upon the harbor. Here were sixteen thousand workmen, constantly employed in replenishing vast magazines with all the different pieces requisite in the construction of vessels; the immense founderies, under the hereditary superintendence of the family of Alberghetti, and, on the same grand scale, the rope-walks in which the best cables in the world were made. The glass-works of Murano furnished mirrors to the vanity of all Europe. The lovers of art found endless delight in the rich paintings, which, although lacking the anatomical accuracy, perspective skill, and comprehensive grandeur of the Florentine school, and the truthful design, matchless grace, and ideal beauty of the Roman, were celebrated for their brilliant coloring and harmonious blending of tints. Rejecting the religious and mystical subjects, the Saints and Madonnas, to which art was usually consecrated, the Venetian painters followed the popular fancy for florid decoration, and immortalized on the walls of St. Mark and in the Ducal Palace the grave senators and voluptuous beauties, the gorgeous festivals and processions that gave to Venice the air of an Oriental city. Bellini had, a hundred years before, adorned the council chamber with the pictured achievements of the proud Republic. Giorgione, his illustrious pupil and the teacher of Titian, had left his masterpiece,

"Christ carrying the Cross," in the Church of St. Roco. Pordenone had painted his frescoes in the Church of St. Stefano, with sword by his side, to protect himself against the jealousy of his rival, the impetuous Titian. Andrea Schiavone, rescued by the latter from the obscurity of sign-painting, was living, and in poverty; for he shared the fate, so often allotted to genius, of contemporary neglect and posthumous praise. Paul Veronese was now at the height of his brilliant reputation, and Palma was embellishing the palace of St. Mark. Zuccaro, who afterwards so splendidly decorated the hall of the Grand Council that he was rewarded with the order of knighthood, was at present in England, painting the portraits of Elizabeth, and some of her courtiers. Yet more conspicuous than these was Tintoretto, whose bold, rapid, fantastic pencil procured for him the sobriquet of "Il Furioso." His efforts to combine Florentine grandeur with Venetian coloring were evidenced in the inscription on the door of his studio, "Il Disegno di Michel Angelo, e il Colorito di Tiziano." His finest picture was that of a Venetian slave, about to suffer martyrdom from the Turks, when St. Mark, the patron saint of the republic, suddenly appears, in answer to her prayers, destroys the instruments of death, and disperses the executioners. But superior to all was Titian, the last and greatest of the Venetian school, now enjoying the mellowed radiance of a serene old age in his palace opposite the island of Murano, at the windows of which he might often be seen at the sunset hour, listening to the songs of the gondoliers, or conversing with the many guests who sought his presence. We may be sure that Philip Sidney visited the illustrious artist who had been honored by kings and lauded throughout Europe; to pick up whose pencil, Charles V. pronounced a service worthy of an emperor, and whose pictures were declared by him to be above all price.

The kindred art of music was the pastime of all the sons of genius. They often met for its enjoyment; and Tintoretto, as Giorgione a few years before, was often persuaded to lend to patrician concerts the peculiar melody of his voice.

Palladio, the famous architect, was still living. Sansovino, the sculptor, had died two years before; but his fame survived in the colossal statues of Neptune and of Mars, and in the decorations of the Mint and Library. Here, too, were men of letters. Tasso, still young, had written his Rinaldo, and was about publishing his Jerusalem. Francis Sansovino and Manutius, the learned printers and classical writers; Paruta, the historian; Paoli Sarpi, subsequently the able defender of Venice in its quarrels with Pius V., were the other celebrities of the day: and we have good reason to believe that Sidney frequently enjoyed the advantages of their society.

The temptations of this gay city to young men of rank and fortune were doubtless manifold, and few of his countrymen escaped their contamination. Roger Ascham, the good preceptor of Lady Jane Grey, lamented the practice of sending the youth of England to reside in Italy; declaring that they returned "sneerers, flatterers, backbiters, tainted with the vices of Venice, atheists, and epicures." But the watchful counsels of Languet, his own æsthetic and literary studies, and especially his pure and elevated principles, preserved Sidney from the evils whose mildew, once fallen on the soul, time and tears only can efface. And here it may be interesting to present to the reader a brief extract on the objects of self-culture, from one of Sidney's works; regarding it as an expression of his habits of thought and study, at all periods of his life.

"This purifying of wit, this enriching of memory, ennobling of judgment and enlarging of conceit, which commonly we call learning; under what name soever it come forth, or to what immediate end soever it be directed, the final end is, to lead and draw us to as high perfection as our degenerate souls (made coarse by their clay lodgings) can be capable of. This, according to the inclinations of man, bred many-formed impressions; for some that thought this felicity principally to be gotten by knowledge, and no knowledge to be so high or heavenly as to be acquainted with the stars, gave themselves to astronomy; others persuading themselves to be demi-gods, if they knew the causes of things, became natural and supernatural philosophers; some, an admirable delight drew to Music; and some, the certainty of demonstrations, to the mathematics; but all, one and other, having this scope, To Know, and by knowledge to lift up the mind from the dungeon of the body, to the enjoying of its divine essence. But when, by the balance of experience, it was found that the astronomer, looking to the stars, might fall into a ditch, that the inquiring philosopher might be blind to himself, and the mathematician might draw forth a straight line with a crooked heart;—then, lo! did Proof, the overruler of opinions, make manifest that all these are but serving sciences; which, as they are all directed to the higher aim of the mistress-knowledge, Knowledge of a Man's Self, in the ethic and politic consideration—with the end of Well Doing, not of well knowing only—so the end of all earthly learning being virtuous action, those skills that most serve to bring forth *that*, have a most just title to be princes over the rest." *

After a few months sojourn in Venice, Sidney withdrew to the quiet and learned city of Padua, that he might devote himself to severe study in the sciences of geometry and astronomy, to Cicero's Epistles, and the works of Plutarch, which were then very rare and with difficulty obtained. He remained there eight months, assiduously storing his mind with the wisdom of the acute and critical Greek, and forming his style upon the classic elegance of the Roman; while his recreation was found in the pages of Petrarch and Boccaccio, of Dante and Ariosto, whose hymns of genius still thrill the pulse of fair but faded Italy.

Of Sidney's correspondence with Languet only seventeen letters have been handed down to us; but they most pleasantly indicate the friendship of these eminent men, their mutual interest in the political transactions of the times, and Sidney's scholastic pursuits under the direction and advice of his learned guide. Here is one dated January 15, 1574:

* Defence of Poesy.

Righte honorable my very good Lorde. I am bolde to troble
your L. withe these few wordes. humbly to craue your Lps
fauour so furr unto me, as that it will please you to lett
me undrestande. whether I may withe your Lps. leaue, and
that I may not offende in wante of my seruice remaine
absente frome the courte this Christmas tyme

Frome wilton this 16th of December 1577

Philippe Sidney.

"Behold at last my letter from Padua! Not that you are to expect any greater eloquence than is usually to be found in my epistles, but that you may know I have arrived here as I proposed, and in safety; and I think it right without any delay to write you a few words from hence, for your satisfaction and my own, as far as communication by letter can be satisfactory. Here I am then, and I have already visited his Excellency the Count and the Baron Slavata, your worthy young friends, and while I enjoy their acquaintance with the greater pleasure to myself, I am perpetually reminded of your surpassing love of me, which you show in taking so much care not only for me, but for all my concerns and conveniences, and that without any deserving on my part. But you are not a man to be thanked for such a thing; for you are even now meditating greater kindness still, and in truth, as far as I am concerned, much as I am indebted to you, I am only too willing to owe you more. . . . . Your last letter brought me no news, for it was filled with instances of your affection, ever pleasant indeed, but long since known and proved, a kind of letter which is, above all others, delightful and acceptable to me, for while I read I fancy that I have the very Hubert himself before my eyes and in my hands. I intend to follow your advice about composition thus: I shall first take one of Cicero's letters and turn it into French; then from French into English, and so once more by a sort of perpetual motion it shall come round into Latin again. Perhaps too I shall improve myself in Italian by the same exercise. For I have some letters translated into the vulgar tongue by the very learned Paolo Manuzio,* and into French by some one else. The volumes of Cicero I will read diligently. There are some things also that I wish to learn of Greek, which hitherto I have skimmed on the surface. But the chief object of my life, next to the everlasting blessedness of heaven, will always be the enjoyment of true friendship, and there you shall have the chiefest place." . . .

On the 4th of February he writes again:—

"Your last letter was, on many accounts, most delightful to me, full as it was of your affectionate regard. I am glad you approve of my intention of giving up the study of astronomy, but about geometry I hardly know what to determine. I long so greatly to be acquainted with it, and the more so, because I have always felt sure that it is of the greatest service in the art of war; nevertheless I shall pay but sparing attention to it, and only peep through the bars, so to speak, into the

* A celebrated printer of Venice.

rudiments of the science. Of Greek literature I wish to learn only so much as shall suffice for the perfect understanding of Aristotle. For though translations are made almost daily, still I suspect they do not declare the meaning of the author plainly or aptly enough; and besides, I am utterly ashamed to be following the stream, as Cicero says, and not go to the fountain head. Of the works of Aristotle, I consider the politics to be the most worth reading; and I mention this in reference to your advice that I should apply myself to moral philosophy. Of the German language, my dear Hubert, I absolutely despair. It has a sort of harshness, (you know very well what I mean,) so that at my age, I have no hope that I shall ever master it, even so as to understand it; nevertheless, to please you, I will sometimes practise it, especially at dinner with my good Delius. I readily allow that I am often more serious than either my age or my pursuits demand; yet this I have learned by experience, that I am never less a prey to melancholy than when I am earnestly applying the feeble powers of my mind to some high and difficult object.

"I am both glad and sorry that you ask me so urgently for my portrait; glad, because a request of this kind breathes the spirit of that sweet and long-tried affection with which you regard me;

and sorry that you have any hesitation in asking me for so mere a trifle." . . "As soon as ever I return to Venice, I will have it done either by Paul Veronese or by Tintoretto, who hold by far the highest place in the art." . . .

His letters in April and May of the same year are replete with anxiety in regard to the prospects of the Protestant cause:—

"I would have you believe that I am deeply and sincerely distressed. For I have heard, and that from no obscure persons, but even from the Council of Ten, that Count Louis has been defeated and mortally wounded; his brother taken, and a great number of his people slain, among whom, most distinguished, are Christopher, son of the Palatine, and certain Counts of the Rhine, as they are called. And they say that such a panic has arisen from this in Belgium, that unless some Christian prince comes to the rescue, affairs are tending to a surrender. I hope, indeed, and hope because I wish, that this is a false rumor, spread about to please the Spaniards, who desire nothing so much as that men should believe they are prospering. But howsoever it may be, my dearest Languet, this at least is certain, that our princes are enjoying too deep a slumber." . . . "I lately saw a work, written with some skill, in which the author strongly urges the princes whom he calls Catholic, to carry out the decrees of the Council of Trent; and he finds occasion for this especially in the disgraceful indolence of the German princes; for while some of them are engaged in carousals, others in absurd hunting parties, others again in turning the course of rivers with lavish expenditure; and all, except the Palatine, have made up their minds to neglect their people and ruin themselves, he is confident they may easily be crushed." . . . "I have written to-day to my uncle, the Earl of Leicester, and have told him all the results which the Spaniards promise themselves from this victory. Perhaps some good may come of my letter, and if not, at any rate, for my own part, I would rather be charged with lack of wisdom than of patriotism." . . . . "I hear the Turks are making great preparations this year, so that I hope the Spaniards will have to think more of defending their own homes than of attacking other men. And hence many persons begin to doubt whether John of Austria will return to Spain. Cosmo, Duke of Florence, died the other day; his people lament him greatly, with the same feelings as those of the woman of Syracuse, who prayed long life to King Dionysius. His successor is even now busily treating with the Turks, that his Etrurian subjects may have free access to trade in Greece."

. . . . . . "I do hope that before many years are past, the virtues of these Spaniards will be understood by the whole world. They were born slaves, and have done nothing ever since (as if to make bad worse) but change their masters; for they have always been servants of Carthaginians, Romans, Vandals, Goths, Saracens, or Moors; of late, indeed, they have been somewhat raised by the character of one man, Charles, and he was a Belgian, and since his death all the world sees with what speed they are hastening back to their original condition." . . . .

The University of Padua was one of the most renowned in this age and country of scholars,* and Philip Sidney must often have met its erudite professors in the salons of the renowned Pinelli. This refined and wealthy gentleman made his house the resort of distinguished men from all parts of the world, and generously opened to them his library, containing every valuable book in print, and his museum of curiosities and of scientific instruments.

Returning to Venice in February, 1574, Sidney

* In Tiraboschi, Storia della Letteratura Italiana, vol. 7, pp. 89–91, will be found a full and interesting account of the condition of the University of Padua during the 16th century. In 1564, two hundred Germans were there studying law; together with many artists, and foreigners from all parts.

wrote to Languet of his purpose to visit Rome. That faithful friend, alarmed it would seem, lest his religious principles should be subverted in the head-quarters of Romish proselytism, sent him repeated and earnest letters of dissuasion, assuring him that a visit there would hazard both his faith and his reputation. "If you should fall into the hands of those robbers at Rome," he writes, "you must either renounce the religion you profess, or expose your life to extreme danger. It would be entirely impossible for you altogether to escape them; for although you might not have reason to be afraid of the treachery of those who pretend to be your friends, yet the dignity of your aspect would cause many to be inquisitive concerning you. What mighty advantage would accrue to you from inspecting for a few days the ruins of Rome, merely to boast that you had seen them? God has granted to you more than to any one I know, an energy of genius, not for the purpose of abusing it, by examining vain objects to your great danger, but of employing it for the advantage of your country and of all good men. You are only the steward as it were of your noble talents, and by the abuse of them you offend against that Being who has conferred such a blessing on you." "Mi dulcissime filii," he adds in another letter, "it is difficult for a man clothed in white apparel to remain in an apartment filled with smoke and dust, without soiling his garment; nor can the complexion which has been long exposed to the sun, retain its native hue. Equally difficult it will be for you to preserve your mind pure and spotless if you converse with the Italians; the inhabitants of Venice and Padua alone excepted, who have not yet entirely degenerated from the simplicity of those nations from which they deduce their origin."

Sidney yielded to the advice of his friend, but expressed regret at a later period of his life that he had not visited the imperial city, and seen with his own eyes the fanes of pagan prayer mouldering among the Christian ideals of Raphael and Angelo; that he had not stood within the shadows of the Coliseum, or meditated among the eloquent sepulchres of the Appian Way.

Paul Veronese was the artist whom Sidney employed about this time to paint his portrait. Languet attributes its sad and thoughtful expression to the severe studies which had occupied his mind, and somewhat impaired his health.

Just before his final departure from Venice, he had the pleasure of witnessing a superb fète given to Henry III. of France, on his way from Poland to Paris. It will be remembered that when Duke of Anjou, he was the hero of Jarnac and Moncontour, successfully opposing, at the age of eighteen, the most marvellous prowess to the veteran skill of the elder Condé and Coligni. We next hear of some hollow-hearted matrimonial negotiations with Elizabeth of England, and then of his active part in the tragedy of St. Bartholomew. The following year, the death of the last brave Jagellon left Poland without a king, and Henry Valois was invited to the empty throne. The splendid pageant of his progress through Germany, and his entrance with an escort of forty thousand richly dressed attendants, was followed by a brief and discontented reign. Disappointed in his kingdom and unpopular with his subjects, on the death of his brother Charles IX., he joyfully threw down the crown already hated, and hastened to assume that of his hereditary realm. Having accepted an invitation to visit Venice on his way, the most elaborate preparations were there made for his reception. A gorgeous galley was built for his especial use, and thirty patrician youth appointed to attend him. The Doge went to meet him in the royal Bucentaur and the dignified body of senators escorted him to the palace of the Foscari. The city resounded with music by day, and blazed with illuminations by night. The venerable Titian received the princely cortège at his palace, and presented the king with several of his paintings. Another day he was conducted to the arsenal, where a mechanical feat was exhibited in the entire construction of a vessel in the space of two hours. A grand banquet was then given on board, at which the knives and forks, plates and napkins were all, with curious inutility, composed of sugar. At a subsequent entertainment in the ducal palace, three hundred groups of lions, nymphs, ships, and griffins, of the same material were gallantly presented to the fair Portias of the occasion.*

Nearly three years had passed away since Philip Sidney's departure from his native land, and he was now impatient to return. They had been years of unwearied research and diligent acquisition, rearing a worthy superstructure upon the basis of his early education. He had learned to converse fluently in the French, Spanish, and Italian languages; he had enriched his mind with classic lore and familiarized it with the literature of the age. From the schools of philosophy he had won the power of subtle thought, from the study of the sciences, that of critical analysis; and in the works of art he had seen embodied the ideals of his own poetic fancy. He had learned

* Daru's Histoire de la République de Venise, 2d ed., Paris, 1821.

lessons of statesmanship and of military life; and prepared himself equally for the perplexing duties of the one, and the arduous action of the other. To all this must be added that irresistible grace which baffles imitation and cannot be described; but which, emanating from the serene religious faith that was with him not only a principle but a feeling, bestowed, as the dew upon the flower, its crowning excellence upon the unfolded beauty of his character.

His homeward route through Germany was rapid, and unmarked by striking incidents. We next hear of his presentation at court under the auspices of his uncle, the Earl of Leicester.

CHAPTER V.

IT would seem almost an impertinence to transfer to new canvas the familiar picture of the England of Shakspeare and the Maiden Queen. But with the knightly figure of Sir Philip Sidney in the foreground, we may be permitted to give prominence to that, by dashing into the background a few slight outlines of some other conspicuous personages of the day. We will drape them in their own attire, and follow them with rapid step from antique mask and revelry to the grave deliberations of the council chamber, to fields of prowess, and seas of adventure. With the dawn of liberal thought lately breaking upon Europe still mingled the reflected light of the fading star of chivalry, and nowhere were gallant feats of arms and courtly observances so essentially blended with statesmanship and valor as among the subjects of the lion-hearted, but beauty-loving, Tudor. Her men of silk were also men of iron. If, one hour, they knelt before her in velvet hose and doublet, and wooed her virgin heart with fantastic adulation and suppliant roundelay of love, the next might see them in martial array, hastening with impatient step to her armies in Holland, or bearing down upon the pirate fleet of Spain, with the war-cry of "England and the Queen!"

In truth, this strange compound of Diana, Semiramis, and Cleopatra, whom men called Elizabeth—this Amazon in will, and almost Sybarite in pleasure, tried the candidates for her service by a lofty and peculiar standard—just that of a politic and sagacious, yet susceptible and exacting, woman. She demanded indomitable courage, but the sword, burning in its scabbard, must wait her signal to unsheathe. Abdiel, the faithful, could hardly have satisfied her with his fidelity, and Bayard would have been required to consecrate his chivalry to her solitary shrine. She valued, like a wise sovereign, patriotism and principle; and she admired, as only a woman can admire, manly beauty and accomplishment. Sir Walter Raleigh found the sacrifice of his costly cloak a stepping-stone, in double sense, to her favor; and Sir Christopher Hatton owed his promotion to the accidents of a handsome person and graceful dancing. The "Gypsey Earl," as swarthy Leicester was called, knew well how to enthral her with the glamour of his dark eyes;

and even her sixty years of withered maidenhood were not proof against the youthful blandishments of Essex. But Sir Christopher would not have danced into the lord-chancellorship, if he had not shown, to her penetrating eye, the ability which the office required; nor could Leicester, with all his beguiling arts, ever make her forget that she carried a crown as well as a heart. Power was, after all, her predominating passion, and though the restless heart would sometimes struggle in its lonely prison, yet the crown of the daughter of Henry the Eighth rested on a brow as proudly defiant as that of her imperious father. With ungenerous perversity, she would neither hazard the matrimonial experiment herself, nor willingly permit any of those in her immediate service to do so. It was happiness enough for her cavaliers to bask in the sunshine of her smiles, and be permitted occasionally to kiss her beautiful hand; and her poor maids of honor soon found that a profession of vestal frigidity was indispensable to a place in her regard. Doubtless the sly flirtations of Greenwich and Richmond received a greater zest from the vigilance of the royal duenna. But although the grave offence of matrimony was often visited by disgrace, and even imprisonment, especially if the offender were a suitor or a kinsman, it is mentioned as a remarkable fact, that Hatton, the superlative dancer, was the only one of her ministers who lived and died a bachelor.

The paradoxical perfections which Elizabeth sought were so singularly blended in most of her eminent men, that it might seem a question whether they were created expressly for her service, or she, to elicit from their singular antagonisms, the strength and power of her administration. It is certain that both were peculiarly adapted to the perils of that political crisis. The eye of Protestantism was anxiously turned upon England, and England knew that only the wisest dexterity could baffle the combined intrigues of the Catholic powers. If they could have released Mary Stuart from her prison, and led her in triumph to the English throne, then might the champions of religious freedom throughout Europe have perished in the dungeons of the Inquisition, or stifled in silence the cry of their despair. The temporizing policy of Elizabeth and her ministers was a difficult but well-wrought problem. It was necessary to intimidate without incensing, to negotiate without self-committal, to attack without suffering reprisal, to retreat without dishonor, to elude the spy and discern the traitor, to aid the weak and defy the strong. Meanwhile the fleet must be enlarged, the militia kept in training, (for England had then no standing army,) the treasury enriched, and the people encouraged.

When Philip Sidney first entered upon the brief career of his manhood, there stood at the helm of state, faithful as Nestor and incorruptible as Aristides, Cecil, Lord Burleigh, once deservedly called by a great man of France, "Quasi Rex et Pater Patriæ." England never rejoiced in a better or a wiser statesman than the Lord Treasurer. Neither personal interest, sickness, misfortune, friend nor foe, could divert him from the affairs of his office when they demanded his attention. Fearless and uncompromising, both liberal and frugal, his mind could grasp the most comprehensive objects, and descend to the most minute. So proudly upright was he that nothing could offend him more than the offer of a bribe. He was said not to have been idle more than half an hour during twenty-four years, and, with impartial justice, he listened as readily to the poor as to the rich. Of commanding presence and winning kindness of manner, this faithful servant was well appreciated by the Queen, although her impetuous temper often visited him with angry words. "I will stoop for your master, but not for the King of Spain," she once said to his servant, when on entering Burleigh's sick chamber, her towering head-dress made such condescension necessary.

Sir Nicholas Bacon, the father of him whose name is a synonyme of both wisdom and weakness, was the second great pillar of the privy council. He was the most acute thinker of them all, and the tangled questions of state were often unravelled by his patient deliberation. "Let us stay a little," he would say, "and we shall have done the sooner."

Leicester played Endymion to England's Diana, ingeniously weaving at the same time various little underplots of love with Diana's nymphs. Arrogant, unscrupulous, and artful, he was the most unpopular of statesmen, and not often essentially serviceable; but his insinuating manners, his lavish ostentation, not unmingled with generosity, and the partiality of the Queen, encircled his head with a perpetual halo. It is but justice to add, that he was a patron of letters, and liberal in gifts to his church, which was of the new sect of Puritans; and that he was always most kind and true to his relatives, especially to his nephew Philip, whom he really loved.

Lord Buckhurst was a faithful and honorable counsellor, but chiefly distinguished for his dramatic and poetic talents, and as the author of Gorboduc, the first tragedy written in the English language, a work highly commended by Pope for its perspicuous and dignified style.

Walsingham was in England, lending to state affairs, as usual, his astute diplomacy and sleepless vigilance. Then there was the brave and honest Lord Hunsdon, first cousin of the queen; somewhat rough in speech, and better pleased with the freedom of the camp than the tiresome punctilios of the court. The preëminently handsome Howard was another royal relative, who, thirteen years later, conducted the attack upon the terrible Armada, and was in consequence created Earl of Nottingham. It was to the wife of this nobleman that Essex entrusted the celebrated ring to which his destiny was linked; and its fatal retention was owing to the personal enmity of the Earl toward the ill-starred favorite.

Conspicuous in the tilt-yard, and eager as Quixote himself in all knightly exercises, was Sir Henry Lee—always the declared champion of her Majesty. He was the founder of the gallant band of Knights Tilters, who, numbering twenty-five of her favorite courtiers, met once a year to exhibit their chivalrous exploits. Another ornament of this romantic society was the Earl of Cumberland, who, at tournaments, proudly wore in his high-crowned hat a glove which was bestowed upon him by the coquettish vestal as he knelt to kiss her hand, and which, with flattering devotion, he immediately caused to be set in diamonds.*

Sir John Perrot, the gigantic Apollo, and fearless soldier, was mostly occupied in Ireland, vainly striving with Sir Henry Sidney to subdue its turbulent inhabitants. Sir Francis Drake was in the same unsatisfactory service, but busily revolving the renowned voyage upon which he entered two years later. Raleigh had lately returned from France, where, for six years past, he, with a company of gentlemen volunteers, had lent his aid to the Huguenots. Though now pretending to study law in the Inner Temple, we must believe that his reveries were far less among its musty folios and parchments, than in the golden enchantments and the orange groves of America. Shakspeare, eleven years old, was picking up a little Latin at the free school in Stratford; and Francis Bacon, a youth of fifteen, was astonishing the professors of Cambridge by his precocious criticisms upon their time-honored philosophy. Then there was Sussex, brave soldier and honorable counsellor, always ready, in any way, to serve his country. Norris, with his five martial

* Petrarch even surpassed the English Earl, for he wrote four sonnets to express the pleasure he received from picking up Laura's glove.

brothers, Sir Francis Vere, Knowles, Cavendish, and a host of others, not forgetting the proud and petulant Lord Oxford, who hereafter recurs to our notice in a little passage-at-arms with Sir Philip Sidney. Heywood, the witty dramatist and popular favorite, had recently died. Camden was writing his Britannia; Stow's Chronicles had just appeared, and Hollinshed's came out the next year. Bishops Jewell and Parker had passed away, not long before; and Hooker, the "judicious" expounder of ecclesiastical law, was young and unnoticed.

History bestows high praise upon the "sweethearts and wives" of England in that era. Strype writes, of the reign of Edward VI., "It is now no strange matter to hear gentlewomen, instead of vain communication about *the moon shining in the water*, use grave and substantial talk in Latin or Greek of godly matters. It is now no news for young damsels in noble houses and in the courts of princes, instead of cards and other instruments of idle trifling, to have continually in their hands either Psalms, Homilies, and other devout meditations, or else Paul's Epistles, or some book of holy Scripture; and as familiarly to read or reason thereof in Greek, Latin, French, or Italian, as in English." Although, twenty-five years later, the court of Elizabeth was marked by strict decorum, there was a decided relaxing, if not from the austere virtues, at least from the solemn occupations, of her brother's reign. We hear marvellous stories of the Queen's reading the Greek Testament daily, and entertaining her maidens with Seneca and Socrates, as they plied the needle in embroidery; and we are told that the daughters of duchesses alternated the classics with the preparation of savory viands and perfumed waters, for medicine or the toilet. But the ladies of the court were doubtless fully occupied with the pageants and processions, the bear-baitings, and excursions in gilded barges on the Thames, the royal progresses from one castle to another, the tourneys and festivals which served to keep the Queen before the people. Everybody is familiar with their fantastic attire; with the huge fardingales and starched * ruffs, the perfumed gloves, with air holes stamped in the palm to release the perspiration, the vast fans of ostrich feathers sunk in handles of gold or silver half a yard long, the

* Stubbes, a sarcastic writer of the 17th century, says of this new innovation: "One arch or piller wherewith the devil's kyngdom of great ruffes is propped, is a certaine kind of liquid matter which they call startche; wherein the devil hath learned them to wash and die their ruffes, which being drie, will stand stiff and inflexible about their neckes."

little mirror hanging from the girdle, and the coquettish love-lock thrown over the shoulder, with a flower fastened to the end. We remember the three thousand dresses and eighty wigs of "Queen Bess," and her judicious reproofs of the extravagance of her subjects; and smile at the inventory of remarkable silks embroidered with birds, beasts, bees, caterpillars, spiders, flies, snakes and grasshoppers, suns and fountains, trees and clouds, and one, allegorically covered with eyes.*

London had only 60,000 inhabitants, and there was consequently a very neighborly feeling among its citizens. The picturesque old timber houses were built with gable roofs, oriel windows, gilt vanes, and immense carved chimney-pieces. Tapestry and wooden panels were giving way to plaster, on which a contemporary writer thus delightedly expatiates: "Beside the delectable whitenesse of the stuffe itself, it is laid on so even and smoothlie, as nothing in my judgment can be done more exactly."

Wealth was displayed in quantities of silver-plate, in mirrors from Venice and clocks from Germany; but carpets had not yet entirely superseded the rushes that littered even palatial floors. The table was divided by a large salt-cellar,

* Nichols's Progresses of Queen Elizabeth.

above which were the seats of honor, the choice viands, and the Muscadel and Hippocras, sparkling in Venice goblets; and below, the humble guests and poor kinsmen were content with ale, and coarser fare. Knives were a recent luxury, and forks still unknown. Dinner was at eleven or twelve, and in country houses dessert was eaten in the garden bowers. Evening prayers came at five or six, supper followed, and the night closed with merry sports or the minstrelsy of blind harpers.*

The streets of London were lighted by individual agency, each family hanging out its lanthorn. The Thames was a clear stream, upon which 4,000 watermen plied their craft. Coaches were not introduced until 1580, and were then regarded as an effeminate innovation. "I wonder," says one of those old writers, "why our nobility cannot in fair weather walk the streets as they were wont; as I have seen the

* An extract from one of Massinger's plays gives us some idea of the prodigality of delicate viands that crowded the tables of the wealthy.

"Men may talk of country Christmasses,
Their thirty pound buttered eggs, their pies of carp's tongues,
Their pheasants drenched with ambergris, the carcasses
Of three fat wethers bruised for gravy, to
Make sauce for a single peacock, yet
Their feasts were fasts, compared to the city's."

Earls of Cumberland, Essex, Shrewsbury, &c., besides those inimitable presidents of courage and valor, Sir Francis Drake, Sir Philip Sidney." The ceremonies, sports, and characters described by Shakspeare, are all faithful transcripts of his own era. St. Paul's Cathedral was the fashionable resort, each day, from ten to twelve, A. M., and from three to six, P. M. There sauntered the Mercutios and Gratianos to sport their jewelled rapiers, to learn the news, (for newspapers, those exhilarating little fountains of gossip, had not appeared,) * to make appointments, to offer challenges for the duello, to barter, and to bribe. Falstaff says of Bardolph, "I bought him at St. Paul's." The middle aisle was the grand arena where gallants displayed their silk cloaks and scented doublets, their Italian lace collars and spangled plumes, their peach-colored hose, fringed

* It is asserted that the first English newspaper was published in London in 1588, and called "The English Mercurie." An extract from one of its early numbers preserved in the British Museum, is as follows: "Yesterday the Scotch Ambassador had a private interview with her Majesty and delivered a letter from his Master, containing the most cordial assurance of adhesion to her Majesty's interests, and to those of the Protestant religion; and the young king said to her Majesty's minister that all the favor he expected from the Spaniards was the courtesy of Polyphemus to Ulysses, that he should be devoured the last."

garters, and golden spurs;—the selections of so many foreign marts as to justify the satire of an artist of that time, who, when painting for Lord Lincoln the costumes of different nations, represented English caprice by the figure of a naked man, perplexedly regarding a pair of scissors and numerous colored fabrics heaped around him.

When quarrels occurred at St. Paul's, or when debtors were pursued, the tomb of Warwick was a sacred asylum. In the churchyard was the principal book sale of London, for book-shops had at that time no existence.*

Rosemary was handed round at funerals. "Here's rosemary, that's for remembrance," says Ophelia. "I pray you, love, remember." Wine was offered in churches after weddings, and theatrical companies performed both then and at christenings. Strolling players, in motley colors, continually paraded the streets of London, and delighted the courtiers. Thornbury tells us that "Ben Jonson played Hieronymo with such a troupe, and in a leather doublet, drove the wagon of stage properties." The theatres were on the rudest principle of construction; the floors were strewed with rushes, the scenery never movable, and ludicrously bad. If a temple or a palace was required, the au

* Drake's "Shakspeare and his Times."

dience were quietly told to *suppose* it. A Thebes or a Troy by the same imaginative power, lay behind a door, on which the name was printed in large letters. "Exit Venus, or if you can, let a chair come down from the top and draw her up."* Ladies were never present at these performances, and the parts of women were acted by boys.† But, as Thornbury says of bear-baiting, "the amusements that could please such minds as Burleigh's and Bacon's, are not to be sneered at in the nineteenth century."

We are tempted to extract from this entertaining writer some curious specimens of the customary language of court and city gallants.

* Knight's Pictorial. Collier's Annals of the Stage.

† Sir Philip Sidney in his Defence of Poesy, thus ridicules the violation of the dramatic unities of time and place,—

"You have Asia of the one side and Africa of the other, and so many other kingdoms that the player when he comes in, must ever begin with telling where he is, or else the tale will not be conceived. Now shall you have three ladies walk to gather flowers, and then we must believe the stage to be a garden. By and by we hear of shipwreck in the same place, then we are to blame if we accept it not for a rock. Upon the back of that comes out a hideous monster with fire and smoke, and then the miserable beholders are bound to take it for a cave; while in the mean time, two armies fly in, represented with four swords and bucklers, and then, what hard heart will refuse to receive it for a pitched field?"

A lady's solitude is invaded by one of these daintily-dressed creatures, who thus addresses her,—"Madam, your beauties being so attractive, I wonder that you are left thus alone."

"Better be alone, Sir, than ill accompanied."

"Naught can be ill, lady, that can come near your goodness, for, sweet Madam, on what part of you soever a man casts his eye, he meets with perfection. You are the lively image of Venus throughout; the graces smile in your cheeks, your beauty nourishes as well as delights. You have a tongue steeped in honey, and a breath like a panther; a cloud is not soft as your skin; your cheeks are Cupid's baths wherein he uses to steep himself in milk and nectar; he does light his torches at your eyes, and instructs you how to shoot and wound with his beams. Yet I love in you nothing more than your innocence; you retain so native a simplicity, so unblamed a behavior. Methinks with such a love I should find no head or foot of my pleasure. You are the very spirit of a lady."

Even this strained affectation gives but a scanty idea of the elaborate ceremonial of the age's politeness.

At the passage of a door you must imagine tedious bowing and shaking of legs, and waving of hats, and,

"'Tis yours, Sir."

"With your example, Sir."

"Not I, Sir!"

"It is your right."

"By no possible means."

"You have the way."

"As I am noble!"

"As I am virtuous!"

"Pardon me, Sir!"

"I will die first!"

"You are a tyrant in courtesy!"

all this to be ended by some one as wise as Master Slender stepping in briskly with,

"I'd rather be unmannerly than troublesome. By your leave, Sir." *

It was etiquette during this reign, for lovers to assume by certain negligences of dress that the tender passion had absorbed their thoughts and driven them to despondency. Rosalind says to Orlando in As You Like It, "There's none of my Uncle's marks upon you; he taught me how to know a man in love. Your hose should be ungartered, your bonnet unbanded, your sleeve unbuttoned, your shoe untied, and every thing about you demonstrating a careless desolation." Yet these men blended with their fantastic

* Thornbury's Shakspeare's England.

knight-errantry the stanch patriotism, the unflinching courage, the religious fervor that would lead them over untried seas to unknown lands, sustain them in the tortures of the Inquisition, and nerve them for the field of battle.

We must not omit to mention another element of the times which tinged with its mystical shadow some ot the wisest minds in Europe. The alchemist still promised to distil from his crucible the philosopher's stone and the elixir of life, Paracelsus was revered in Germany, and Dr. Dee, the astronomer and geometrician, cast nativities under the patronage of Leicester and the Queen. A hundred years before, it was asserted in Germany that the product of burned Jews would be pure gold, twenty-four bodies being equivalent to ten pounds of the precious metal; and even in 1600, Bacon and Shakspeare spoke with respect of astrologic art and planetary influences.

And now, in the midst of this picturesque generation, we see again the accomplished and loyal gentleman, for whose sake we have called up its retreating shadows. Philip Sidney was one of those persons who seem unconsciously to wield a strange magnetism over every one around them —whose silence even speaks, and whose atmosphere is redolent of a subtle charm that may be felt but not analyzed, remembered but not comprehended. In the language of Fuller we are told, "he became so essential to the English Court that it seemed maimed without his company." Whether discoursing with serene old Burleigh and dark-browed Walsingham, or throwing the lance with Cumberland and Lee, or repeating, in his low, musical tones, (for his voice was one of surpassing sweetness,) stories of Venice and Vienna to the listening maids of honor, his was ever the happy presence that irradiated and cheered.

> "Was never eie did see that face,
> Was never eare did heare that tonge,
> Was never minde did minde his grace,
> That ever thought the travell long;
> But eies, and eares, and ev'ry thought,
> Were with his sweet perfections caught."
>
> *Spenser's Astrophel.*

The nephew of Leicester was sure of a gracious reception from the Queen; but her penetration soon discerned his higher claims to her regard, and, as a preliminary to future honors from her hand, she appointed him to the courtly office of her cupbearer. It was a part of her romantic eclecticism, a mixture perhaps of policy and preference, to employ the gravest statesmen and most finished cavaliers in trifling services about her sacred person; and such duties were performed by them with the devotion of knights-templars on a crusade.

A few months after Sidney's return to England, he took part in one of those dazzling pageants which have been reflected for us in the magic mirror of Sir Walter Scott. The Queen had bestowed upon Lord Leicester the princely gift of Kenilworth, and sometimes honored him with a visit there; but the favored subject, having lately expended £60,000 in enlarging and adorning it, again besought her presence for a few days. In various pages of pompous declamation, we are told how a gay cavalcade of belted knights and lovely ladies, numbering in all some two or three hundred, glittered along the broad avenues, and wound up the sloping hill, one warm July evening; and as the warder's horn resounded from the battlements, the greeting shouts of retainers and bursts of joyous music welcomed to the brave old Saxon castle the illustrious daughter of a long race of kings. It were tedious to attempt a repetition of the gorgeous phantasmagoria that crowded those festal days, and transformed an English home into a mythological museum. The Fauns and Satyrs of buried heathenism suddenly peopled its groves, and bent reverently to the Christian Venus; mermaids emerged with dripping locks from the waters of its lake, to salute her with laudatory rhymes; Pan and Bacchus poured libations at her feet. On a temporary bridge, seventy feet in length, thrown from the court to the main building, stood seven Grecian divinities, who offered, on her arrival, various grotesque presents—fruits, fishes, cages of birds, silver bowls of grapes and wine, musical instruments, suits of armor, &c. explanations of which were given in Latin verse by a poet, clad in light blue silk. The castle clocks were stopped at the moment of her arrival, as if Time itself were in royal waiting. Dancing and revels occupied each evening, while the discharge of cannon echoed through the grounds, and fireworks flashed amid the venerable trees. A water pageant exhibited the lady of the lake on an illuminated island, and a huge dolphin glided over the waves, with Arion singing on his back, and an orchestra of twenty-four men making music within his body.* The refined diversion of bear-baiting, which even gentle women then looked upon with pleasure, hunting the stag, tournaments, and masques, crowded nineteen days of laborious amusement.

We will here give a specimen of the last-named performance, in a brief synopsis of the *Lady of May*, which was written by Philip Sid-

* Laneham's Kenilworth.

ney, at the request of his uncle, when the Queen visited his Castle of Wanstead. Though absurdly insipid to modern taste, we must remember that Shakspeare was yet unheard of, and the English theatre, in its crude beginning.

Her Majesty, while walking through a grove, is suddenly accosted by one of the maskers dressed as a farmer's wife, who falls upon her knees and informs her that her daughter is addressed by two suitors, of such equally divided merits that she finds it impossible to choose between them ; and lest the rapidly increasing jealousy of the lovers should meet a fatal termination, she entreats the Queen to act as umpire. Leaving an adulatory poem in her Majesty's hands, she disappears, and there emerge from the wood a dozen shepherds and foresters, accompanied by the prize of contention, the Lady of May. They are all smitten with admiration at the royal presence, and one of them, who is a schoolmaster, delivers an exceedingly inflated speech,* plentifully

* Many of the writers of this reign were imbued with a love of antithesis and declamation, of mythological allusions and far-fetched metaphors. One of the most noted of this school was Lilly, whose "Euphues" became the standard of imitation and of courtly parlance, "she who spoke not Euphuism being as little regarded as if she could not speak French." Sir Philip ridicules the affectation, in the character

sprinkled with Latin, in which he repeats the story of the damsel's mother. The Lady of May very sensibly interrupts him with the exclamation, "Away, you tedious fool, you are not worthy to look to yonder princely sight, much less your foolish tongue to trouble her wise ears." She then descants upon her lovers and compares their merits, saying in conclusion, "Now the question I am to ask you, is, whether the many deserts and many faults of Therion, or the small deserts and no faults of Espilus, be preferred." The two swains here enter upon a spirited poetical combat, expressive of their devotion to their ladye love, and their detestation of each other Espilus then kneels to the Queen and sings,

> "Judge you, to whom all beauty's force is lent,"

and Therion adds,

> "Judge you of Love, to whom all love is bent."

Hereupon the shepherds fall into a hot dispute in regard to the rival candidates, in which Rombus, the pompous schoolmaster, again engages. The rustic farce closes with the Queen's decision in favor of Espilus, followed by a full chorus from the band, and a song of joy from the grateful swain.

of Rombus, this schoolmaster, as did Shakspeare, subsequently, in the Holofernes of Love's Labor Lost.

But while, with dignified grace, Philip Sidney bore a part in these fantastic ceremonials, his thoughtful mind turned to far different themes. Across the waters of the North Sea swept the heroic shouts of the armies of the Netherlands, and from Germany and France floated, in thrilling tones, the cry of the oppressed. The ear of Sidney listened, and his heart panted for action. Taught from childhood to revere the Protestant faith, his reverence was sublimed to love, and baptized with undying fire, on the sacrificial altar of St. Bartholomew. His association for three years with the Protestants of the continent, his intimacy with Hubert Languet, and his own lofty sense of justice, continually deepened his sympathy and zeal. He knew that the conflict was not for religion only. It was for political, social, and mental emancipation from a tyranny which wound its serpent folds around both soul and substance, stifling the senses and stupefying the brain. He remembered that this was the third great insurrection of free thought against papal domination. The bones of the Albigensian martyrs, bleaching in the valleys of the south of France, told the hopeless story of the first; the fires that consumed Huss and his disciples were the fierce holocaust of the second; and he felt that the present struggle was the most desperate, the most important, and perhaps the last. A glorious battle-ground invited the young and brave of Europe; the competitors were kings and kingly men; the prizes were liberty, fame, and the benedictions of those whom their prowess should make free. It was hard for an enthusiastic, high-souled man to tinkle the guitar for ladies' pleasure, while the laurels of such a field awaited the brow of the victor—to throw the lance in jesting tourney, while, across a narrow sea, the champions of Truth contended in the lists of life and death. It was once well said, "the duties of life are more than life itself;" and perhaps no part of Sidney's character gleams with a brighter moral than his patient self-control and manly acquiescence, through long years of waiting upon the caprice of his arbitrary Queen. His repeated solicitations for employment abroad were met, as will be hereafter shown, by repeated refusals. "She would not further his advancement," says Naunton,* "because she feared to lose the jewel of her times."

In the year 1576, however, she sent him on an embassy to the court of Vienna, to condole with the new Emperor Rodolph II. on the death of his father Maximilian, and to congratulate him on his own accession. This, at least, was the

* Fragmenta Regalia.

ostensible object of the embassy; the real object was to effect a coalition between England and the Protestant states of Germany against the Catholic powers. We are told that Elizabeth, with her usual pride of externals, had much regard to the handsome face and figure of her ambassador, but she also saw, as did Walsingham and Burleigh, that among the young sons of England they could not find another who united the persuasive address, the integrity and talent requisite for a mission of delicate diplomacy in a foreign land. He departed with a splendid retinue, and travelled in great state through Germany. On all the houses which he occupied, there was affixed a tablet bearing the arms of his family and the following grandiloquent inscription:—

Illustrissimi et generosissimi viri
Philippi Sidnaei Angli,
Pro-regis Hiberniae filii, comitis Warwici,
Et Leicestriae nepotis, serenissimae
Reginae Angliae ad Cesarem legati.*

* Of the most noble and illustrious
Philip Sidney of England,
Son of the Governor of Ireland, kinsman of Warwick,
And nephew of Leicester, Ambassador
To the Emperor of Germany from her Serene Highness
The Queen of England.

The new emperor received him with great courtesy, listening graciously to the messages of royal sympathy on the demise of "that excellent sovereign, his Father," mingled with expressions of hope that his own reign would be equally wise and prudent. His reply, which was in Latin, briefly avowed his intention to imitate the paternal example, and his grateful sense of the attention of the English Queen.

The next day Sidney had an interview with the empress, the widow of Maximilian. Of that, and of his adroit accomplishment of one of the objects of his mission, he thus writes in an official letter to Walsingham:—

"I delivered her Majesty's letter to the Empress, with the singular signification of her Majesty's great good will unto her, and her Majesty's request of her to advise her son to a wyse and peaceable governmente. Of the Emperor deceasea I used but few wordes, because in troth I saw it bredd some troble unto her, to hear him mentioned in that kinde. She answered me with many courteouse speeches, and greate acknowledging of her own beholdingnesse to her Majestie. And for her son, she said, she hoped he wold do well, but that for her own parte, she had given herselfe from the world, and woolde not greatly sturr from thenceforward in it. Then did I deliver the

Queen of Fraunce's letter, she standing by the Empresse, using such speeches as I thought were fitt for her double sorrow, had her Majesty's good will unto her confirmed by her wise and noble governynge of herself in the tyme of her being in Fraunce. Her answer was full of humbleness, but she spake so low that I coulde not understande many of her wordes.*

"From them I went to the yonge princes, and past of each syde certaine complimentes, which I will leave, because I feare me I have alreddy bene overlonge there. The rest of the daies that I lay there, I informed myself as well as I coolde of such particularities as I received in my instructions; as 1, of the Emperor's disposition, and his brethren; 2, By whose advice he is directed; 3, When it is likely he should marry; 4, What princes in Jermany are most affected to him; 5, In what state he is left for revenews; 6, What good agrement there is betwixt him and his

* This good and beautiful daughter of Maximilian II. was married to Charles IX. in 1570, and Sidney was consequently known to her in Paris. She must have discovered in her sanguinary husband that spark of the divine said to exist in the most diabolical characters, for her attachment to him was enduring and sincere. Having promised him on his deathbed never to marry again, she soon after built a convent and there spent the remainder of her life.

brethren; 7, And what partage they have. In these thinges I shall at my returne more largely be liable and with more leysure to declare it. Now only this much I will troble you withe, that the Emperor is wholly by his inclination given to the warres, few of wordes, sullain of disposition, very secrete and resolute, nothinge the mannerse his father had in winninge men in his behaviour, but yet constant in keeping them; and such a one, as, though he promise not much outwardly, but as the Latins say, *aliquid in recessu;* his brother Earnest much lyke him in disposition, but that he is more franke and forward, which perchaunce the necessity of his fortune argues him to be; both extremely Spaniolated."

Sidney rightly divined the character of Rodolph II., who proved himself an unworthy successor to his humane and accomplished father. A bigoted Catholic, and utterly neglectful of the duties of a sovereign, he divided his time between his laboratory and his stables—yet never mounting his horses, which were numerous and magnificent. Tycho Brahe having cast his horoscope and predicted his death by the hand of his own son, he foreswore marriage, and slept in a room barred like a prison of state.

After leaving Vienna, Sidney visited at Heidelburg the Elector Palatine, a brother of Rodolph. He writes again: "I had from her Majesty to condole with the Elector, and to perswade him to unite with his brother."—"One thing I was tolde to add in my speeche, to desyre him in her Majesty's name, to have merciful consideration of the church of the religion so notably established by his father, as in all Jermany, there is not such a number of excellente learned men, and truly it woold rue any man to see the desolation of them. I laide before him as well as I coolde, the dangers of the mightiest princes of Christendom, by entering into lyke violent changes—the wronge he should doe his worthy father, utterly to abolish that he had instituted, and so, as it were, condemne him, besydes the example he shoolde give his posterity to handle him the like."

Returning through the Netherlands, Sidney made the personal acquaintance of the greatest man of that age of greatness,—the pillar of light to the cloud-wrapped hosts of Holland,—William of Orange. It were needless to speak at length of the grand virtues, and the patriotic achievements, which have lately been made universally familiar in the spirit-stirring pages of the "Rise of the Dutch Republic." Sidney had followed them from afar with admiring veneration, and now, as he looked upon the care-worn figure in its severely simple garb, and on the benignant face which anxiety had furrowed at forty-three, the lighter adornments of inferior men seemed to melt away before the calm, comprehensive strength of this matchless character. He had the happiness, not merely of his acquaintance, but of his cordial friendship; and the loftiest tribute to Philip Sidney was that paid by William the Silent, when he called him, with habitual love and deference, "My Master," and pronounced him "one of the ripest and greatest counsellors of that day in Europe." * They never met again, but corresponded for several years on current political affairs. It is much to be regretted that none of these letters can now be discovered.

History may be searched in vain for a more discordant contrast to the hero of Orange, than Don John of Austria, the Spanish Governor of the Low Countries. From the cradle to the grave, the life of this gay, ambitious, fascinating adventurer was one of perpetual romance. He owed his talents to his father, the Emperor Charles V.; his beauty and his boldness to his mother, a laundress of Ratisbon. Reared by a peasant in Spain, he never dreamed that imperial blood coursed through his veins, until, at the age of fourteen, while witnessing a royal hunt, he was

* Fulke Greville's Life of Sidney.

astonished by a brotherly embrace from Philip II., and the assurance of his own august birth. A careful education developed his physical and mental capacities, and, at the age of twenty-three, he was one of the handsomest, haughtiest, and most accomplished men in Europe. His military career began in Granada, where for two years he carried on a crusade less glorious than vindictive. In 1571, the guns of Lepanto echoed his fame throughout the world, and the brilliant courage which won the greatest naval victory of modern times, became the terror of the Turks and the admiration of Christendom. In the elation of success, he made a descent upon Barbary, captured Tunis, and demanded from the Pope the crown and title of king. Philip II., alarmed at the ambition of his kinsman, defeated the application, and hoped to engage his dangerous energies among the insurgents of the Netherlands. But the young Crusader was now busy with another of those selfish and subtle fantasies that for ever occupied his brain. He resolved, by prowess or by plot, to open the prison doors of Mary Queen of Scots, to marry the beautiful captive, dethrone Elizabeth, and rule over the united realms. Many were the high-born hearts that yielded to the strangely captivating knight; and cavaliers, seeking to imitate the careless grace with which the massive brown ringlets were thrown back from his temples, called the fashion by his name. Next to the games of love and war, chess was his favorite, played with living men, who were dressed in the uniforms of different nations.

The haughty Spaniard had no love for Englishmen, and when their young Envoy, untitled, and unheralded by daring deeds, was presented to him at Brussels, it was not to be supposed that his greeting would be very cordial. But even Don John's supercilious coldness vanished before that mingled dignity and sincerity of manner, which were felt by all of Sidney's contemporaries, and which not even the jealous and malignant could refuse to admire.*

> "Ne spight itself, that all good things doth spill,
> Found aught in him that she could say was ill."

The life of this last and most brilliant of the crusaders was a succession of splendid failures. His military exploits against the Moors and Turks were rewarded by neither wealth nor power. He was denied the sovereignty of Tunis; he failed in his romantic scheme of marrying Mary of Scotland, and of ascending with her the double throne; he was utterly foiled in

* Fulke Greville.

the Netherlands by the want of troops and money, and by the superior tactics of William of Orange. In 1578, disappointed, heart-broken, and consumed by fever and fatigue, he wrote with touching pathos to Andrea Doria of Genoa, "They have cut off our hands, and we have now nothing for it but to stretch forth our heads also to the axe."—"I consider you most fortunate that you are passing the remainder of your days for God and yourself."—"I hope that you will remember me in your prayers, for you can put your trust where, in former days, I never could place my own."

A few days later, the hero of Lepanto fought the last battle of earth, after a brief illness, in which, like Napoleon, his delirious fancy again crowned him the head of glittering squadrons, and thrilled his ear with the triumphant shouts of victory. His death was attributed to poison, and grave suspicions rest upon Philip II., who certainly was none too scrupulous, or too good, to render the charge improbable.*

* Some Protestant rhymester, with more zeal than inspiration, published a long monody upon his death, called "The Pope's Lamentation." We extract a few verses:

"O Heaven! O Earth! O Elaments!
 and all therein containde;
Lament with me, poure forth your plaints,
 just cause hath so constrained;

Philip Sidney was complimented by several splendid presents during his absence—among

Sith cursed Death, in cruel wise,
  hath reft me my delight;
Don Joan of Austria, he that sought
  By all the means he might,
To save my Church, and me from harme,
  To strengthen my estate;
And with his power to punish those
  that did my doings hate.
Come, come, my careful Cardnalles now,
  my Prelates and the rest,
That wonted were to wish me well,
  I pray you all be prest,*
To waile with woe the want of him,
  that during tearme of life
Neglected naught that might be wrought,
  to make our glory rife;
Alas! how am I gript with grief,
  what cares do compasse me,
For losse of him whom I ordainde
  My champion cheefe to be;
And therefore Death! I curse thee now,
  and eke thy cruel dart,
Which did to that renowned Prince
  thy poysoned power impart,
Those Huguenots thou mightest have hitte,
  to pacifyre thine yre;
And let this worthy wight alone
  to further my desyre," &c.

* Ready.

others, was a massive gold chain from the Emperor Rodolph, and another, fastened with a jewel, from the Prince of Orange. Of more value were the golden opinions which he won by his rare endowments, and the wisdom and dexterity with which he accomplished the objects of his mission. Even Burleigh, who was unfriendly to Leicester, and not disposed to like any of his relations, bestowed on him the highest praise. This is all pleasantly told in a letter from Walsingham to Sir Henry Sidney. "Now touching your Lordship's particular, I am to impart unto you the return of the young gentleman, your sonne, whose message verie sufficientlie performed, and the relatinge thereof, is no less gratefullye received, and well liked of her Majestie, than the honourable opinion he hath left behinde him with all the princes with whome he had to negotiate, hathe left a most sweet savor and grateful remembraunce of his name in those parts. The gentleman hath given no small arguments of great hope, the fruits whereof I doubt not your Lordship shall reape, as the benefitt of the good parts that are in him, and whereof he hath given some taste in this voyage, is to redounde to more than your Lordship and himself. There hath not ben any gentleman, I am sure, these many yeres, that hathe gon through so honourable a charge with as great commendacions as he; In consideration wherof, I could not but communicate this part of my joy with your Lordship, being no less refreshinge unto me in these my troublesome business, than the soil is to the chased stagge. And so wishing the increase of his good parts to your Lordship's comfort, and the service of her Majestie and his countrie, I humbly take my leave. From the court at Greenwich this Xth of June, 1577.

"Your Lordship's assured friend,

"FRANCIS WALSINGHAM."

CHAPTER VI.

WHEN through the lens of literature we look down the long dim aisles where glide the shadows of the mighty dead, it often happens that the eye is arrested by some form illustrious in the past. As we gaze and ponder, it becomes more luminous and distinct, until it stands before our quickened spirit as a living presence. The exile from earth seems to meet us on the bridge that spans with airy arch the gulf between two worlds. The long silent voice thrills our ear, and from beneath the lifted lid gleams the divine essence. But if we would daguerreotype for other eyes the image that enchants our own, it seems to shrink from the material mirror, and with calm majesty to rebuke the portraiture. Thus we fail to describe what we clearly see; our clumsy camera gives no just reflection; still our love and reverence plead for the effort, although we know that it must be imperfect and unsatisfactory. It is deeply to be regretted that the biographers of Philip Sidney have bequeathed to us so few of those words and deeds which serve as outlines for a portrait. They tell us how, in general terms, he was the pride and marvel of the great and wise; how young gallants aped his fashions and quoted his sayings, and how the hearts of lovely maidens fluttered with pleasure at his approach. It is supposed by some that Shakspeare thought of Sidney, when he wrote of Hamlet,

> "The courtier's, scholar's, soldier's eye, tongue, sword,
> The expectancy and rose of the fair state;
> The glass of fashion, and the mould of form,
> The observed of all observers."

But, though lavish of general praise, these niggard annalists have given us none of those pleasant trifles that glow with vitality—the table-talk, the confiding household undisguises, the straws of anecdote, that show which way the mood moves. For this deficiency we weave through our story a thread of perpetual lament.

Nevertheless, through these vague generalities we often see a lambent gleam of character; such, for example, as is manifest in the brief account of Sir Philip's defence, soon after his return from Germany, of his father's administration in Ireland. Sir Henry had become unpopular there by levying (with undue rigor as it was said) a tax for the maintenance of his own household, and of her Majesty's troops; and the representations made to the Queen had much excited her displeasure. With all the fervor inspired by filial affection, and an indignant sense of wrong, Sidney collected the articles of accusation, and, in a bold refutation, triumphantly vindicated the honor of his father, and effectually restored to him the royal regard.

From this generous zeal arose an incident which has been mentioned, as the sole blot upon an otherwise faultless history. Having learned that through some hidden spy the secrets of Sir Henry had been betrayed, he said to his father, "I must needs impute it to some about you, that there is little written from you or to you, that is not perfectly known to your professed enemies." Suspicion fell upon Edward Mollineux, the friend and secretary of Sir Henry, and the result was the following letter:

"Mr. Mollineux,

"Few woordes are best. My letters to my father have come to the eyes of some; neither can I condemne any but you for it. If it be so, you have plaide the very knave with me, and so I will make you know, if I have good proofe of it; but that for so much as is past; for that is to come, I assure yow before God, that if ever I knowe you to do so much as to reede any lettre I wryte to my father, without his commandment, or my consente, I will thruste my dagger into yow; and truste to it, for I speake it in earnest. In the mean tyme, farewell.

By me,

PHILIPPE SIDNEY."

It is probable that the charge here conveyed was groundless; but if it were true, as Sidney believed it to be, it seems to us that, judged by the standard of his age, and by his own high sense of honor, this curt and pointed epistle finds sufficient palliation. In the category of dishonor, next to an actual betrayal of trust, should be ranked such an act of meanness as extorted this indignant rebuke; nor can the menace surprise us from one who felt, to use his own lofty words, that "death is a less evil than betraying a trusting friend." Besides, when the rapier and the sword were girded in the belt of every cavalier, not only for ornament, but for use, and thrusts and cuts were things of light exchange; and when the Queen herself did not scruple to box the ears of her lords in waiting, or to strike and pinch her maids of honour, it seemed rather creditable to Sidney that, instead of personal altercation, he expressed at the outset, with the frankness of a true gentleman, his displeasure at the offence, and his determination to avenge its repetition.

Sir Henry Sidney was very proud and happy in his favorite son. He writes of him about this time to Robert, his second son, then travelling on the continent: "Follow the advice of your loving brother, who in loving you, is comparable with me, or exceedeth me. Imitate his virtues, exercises, studies and actions; he is a rare ornament of his age, the very formular that all well-disposed young gentlemen of our court do form also their manners and life by. In truth, I speak it without flattery of him or myself, he hath the most virtues that ever I found in any man. I saw him not these six months, little to my comfort. Once again I say, imitate him."

A letter in the Sidney papers from Philip to his brother, so pleasantly indicates his fraternal affection, that one or two extracts cannot fail to be read with interest. Speaking in one of them of his readiness to furnish pecuniary aid, he says, "There is nothing I spend so pleaseth me as that which is for you. If ever I have ability, you will find it; if not, yet shall not any brother living be better beloved than you of me." After many kind admonitions in regard to his studies, among which he advises him to keep a common-place book for making extracts, he adds, "Now, sweet brother, take a delight to keep and increase your music. You will not believe what a want I find of it in my melancholy times."—"I would, by the way, your worship would learn a better hand. You write worse than I; and I write evil enough. Once again have a care of your diet, and consequently of your complexion."—"You purpose, being a gentleman born, to furnish yourselfe with the knowledge of such things as may be serviceable for your country and calling; which certainly stands not in the change of air (for the warmest sun makes not a wise man); no, nor in learned languages, (although they be of serviceable use,) for words are but words, in what language soever they be; and much lesse in that all of us come home full of disguisements, not only of apparel, but of our countenances, (as though the credit of a traveller stood all upon his outside,) but in the right informing your mind with those things that are most notable in those places which you come into. For hard sure it is to know England, without you know it by comparing it with some other country; no more than a man can know the swiftness of his horse without seeing him well matched." Then follows some advice about the use of weapons, "to exercise your health and strength, and make you a strong man at the Tourney and Barriers. First in any case practice with the single sword and afterwards with the dagger. Let no day pass without an hour or two such exercise; the rest study and confer diligently, and so shall you come home to my comfort and credit. Lord! how I have babbled; once again, farewell, dearest brother."

The subject of these letters, though nearly forgotten in the overshadowing fame of his elder brother, became a distinguished man. He received high commendations while travelling on the continent, and secured the friendship of Languet. He was honored with knighthood for his military prowess in the Netherlands, and, some time after, successively created Baron of Penshurst, Viscount l' Isle, and Earl of Leicester. The celebrated Algernon Sidney was his son.

We are told in "Old England's Worthies" that there is preserved at Penshurst "an exceedingly interesting picture by Gerardi, which represents the brothers standing side by side, their arms linked together, the one looking the Protector, and the other the Protected."

There was another brother, named Thomas, of whom little is known, except that he was a valiant military officer.

Mary, Countess of Pembroke, was the only sister of Philip Sidney, and they seem to have been deeply and mutually attached. She is lauded by many writers, in both prose and verse, as a lady of surpassing loveliness and intellectual attainments. Ben Jonson's familiar epitaph we have quoted, and Spenser speaks of her as

> "Urania, sister unto Astrophel,
> In whose brave mind, as in a golden coffer,
> More rich than pearls of Ind, or gold of Ophir,
> And in her sex more wonderful and rare."

We come now to the most important act of Sidney's life, one whose consequences, immediate and remote, upon England, and perhaps upon Europe, were of incalculable extent,—as slight obstructions sometimes change forever the current of a mighty stream. This was the writing of a letter to the Queen, dissuading her from a projected alliance with the heir presumptive of the crown of France. To explain the story clearly, we must go back seven years, to the time when Henry Valois, finding himself unconquerably averse to a union with the august spinster, nineteen years older than himself, suddenly broke away from the matrimonial web, much to the vexation of his mother, and the mortification of the jilted *fiancée*. But Catherine de Medici never gave up a game while a single card remained to play. Anjou had failed, but Alençon, her youngest son, remained. Nostradamus, the famous astrologer, had predicted that her four sons should all be crowned heads, and to verify the prophecy, one of them must espouse the Queen of England. Accordingly, La Motte Fenelon, the French ambassador, resident at London, was instructed to present the overtures of the younger prince. Never were the arts of flattery better practised than by this most insinuating and adroit of Frenchmen ; and never, despite the good sense and dignity which she manifested in many respects, was sovereign more susceptible to these arts than Elizabeth.

The satisfied credulity with which, for ten years, she received the adulation of her boyish suitor and his envoys, and the diplomatic wariness and cunning manifested on both sides, constitute one of the most amusing passages in history. There is no probability that she seriously thought of marrying a man twenty-three years younger than herself, puny in stature, repulsively ugly, deeply marked with smallpox, and so weak and wicked, that his own sister, Marguerite of Valois, said of him, that "if fraud or cruelty were to be banished from the earth, there was in him a stock sufficient to replenish the void." His personal defects were sufficient objection with a princess so fastidious as to have once refused the place of gentleman-usher to an individual who simply lacked one tooth, and who required that, in her walks and rides, all deformed and diseased persons should be carefully kept out of her sight. But this little romance was only another specimen of the political craft and feminine vanity which were blended in most of her actions. It not only furnished occasion to her courtiers to delight her ear with ingenious variations upon her own loveliness, but served to divert France from forming an offensive alliance against her, with Philip II. or the Pope. It also agreeably occupied her discontented Catholic peers, as, from the sullen solitude of their castles, they wistfully looked for the release of Mary of Scotland, or for some other event which should give them a sovereign of their own faith. The proposed match was extremely unpopular with the Protestants; although Sussex, Hunsdon, Admiral Lincoln, and a few others, were its advocates, from the fear of Catholic combination against Elizabeth, and in favor of Mary Stuart. Burleigh, with his usual sagacious prevision, encouraged it, and even borrowed from astrology a persuasive prophecy in its favor—thinking, all the while, that the queen would be amused with this harmless dalliance until it was too late for her to marry at all, and fully determined that such should be the result. A very shrewd old man was the Lord Treasurer; and a stormy time he had in managing his wilful mistress, and in steering the ship of state safely through the breakers and shoals which obstructed its course. The tactics of Elizabeth were first displayed in a demur to the disparity of age, and in the reported absence of beauty in her proposed spouse. Fenelon was armed for all objections. He reminded her that Pepin le Bref only reached to the girdle of his wife, Bertha of Almain, and yet their son Charlemagne was nearly seven feet in height. As to the traces of the smallpox, they would soon be hidden by a beard, or perhaps removed by medical art; and his youth was a decided advantage, since he could be the more easily governed by herself and her councillors. Then followed marvellous representations of the ardor of this doughty knight, and frequent letters from his own hands, replete with reverent adoration. But, at the end of six years of cajoling and evasion, the consummation seemed as distant as ever; and so "Monsieur," as the English called the Prince, (now the Duke of Anjou,) sent over a special pleader in the person of M. Simier. This was another of the brilliant butterflies whom the queen liked to have fluttering about her, and so witty and agreeable did he prove, that she invited him constantly to her private parties, and even received him into her confidence. On all these occasions, he urged with great dexterity the suit of his master, pathetically picturing his melancholy suspense, and his chivalrous devotion to the ladye of his love. At last, one balmy day in June, while this modern Diana sat placidly among her lords and ladies in Greenwich Palace, there knocked loudly at the gates, an unknown knight, in close disguise, who craved admission to her presence. The Duke himself, having, with the romance of a crusader, crossed the channel with only two attendants, now came to learn definitively the result of his long and tedious wooing. The Queen was enchanted. Not one of the royal Jasons in quest of the golden prize had ever before courted her in person; neither Rodolph of Austria, nor the Archduke Charles, Eric of Sweden, Philip of Spain, nor Henry of Anjou. This bold suitor had outdone them all, and, despite the smallpox and the ugly nose, seemed likely to outdo them still. During the few days of his stay, he made such an impression upon the susceptible maiden of forty-six summers, that, a few weeks later, she assembled her council to deliberate upon the proposed alliance. After much grave consultation, mingled with some blunt asides about "old maids," and unsuitable ages, which were very happily not overheard by the venerable coquette, they requested to be "informed of her pleasure on the subject, and they would endeavor to make themselves conformable to it." This was by no means a satisfactory reply. She was decidedly bewitched with Monsieur, and anxious to receive the sanction of her subjects to a union with him. So with a flood of passionate tears she told her ministers that she had expected they would show themselves highly pleased with such remote foreshadowings of an heir to the crown as her marriage might reasonably promise; and with that she gave them a petulant dismissal. She was in very bitter mood for several days. "The sun does not shine," said Hatton; "it is no time to present a petition." The discontent of her subjects could not be concealed; her counsellors gravely demurred, and altogether there was a great struggle between her queenly wisdom and her womanly will. At this uncomfortable crisis, she asked the advice of Philip Sidney, and no doubt expected from the "Jewel of the Times," as she styled him, such courtly counsel as would both soothe and encourage her. His reply was marked by a fearless independence and excellent sense which have commanded for it universal approval. Hume says it was written "with unusual elegance of expression, as well as force of reasoning," and Miss Aiken pronounces it "the most eloquent and most courageous piece of that nature which the age can boast."

With loyal courtesy, he addresses her as his "most feared and beloved, most sweet and gracious sovereign;" refers to conversations he had formerly held with her on the subject of her marriage, in which she had protested that "no private passion or self-affection," could lead her to it; and says, "Now resteth to consider what be the motives of this sudden change, as I have heard you in most sweet words deliver." After alluding to the two religious factions in her kingdom, and reminding her that the security of her own position depended entirely on the affection of her Protestant subjects, to whom she had given the "free exercise of eternal truth," he says, "How will their hearts be galled, if not aliened, when they shall see you take a husband, a Frenchman and a Papist, in whom (howsoever fine wits may find further dealings or painted excuses) the very common people well know this: that he is the son of a Jezebel of our age; that his brother made oblation of his own sister's marriage, the easier to massacre our brothers in belief; that he himself, contrary to his promise and all gratefulness, having his liberty and principal estate by the Huguenots' means, did sack La

Charité, and utterly spoil them with fire and sword! This, I say, even at first sight, gives occasion to all truly religious, to abhor such a master, and diminish much of the hopeful love they have long held to you."

"The other faction," he adds, "is the Papists: men whose spirits are full of anguish, on various accounts; men of great numbers, of great riches, and of united minds. This rank of people want nothing so much as a head, who, in effect, needs not but to receive their instructions, since they may do much mischief only with his countenance." In strong terms, he pictures the enmity of the Catholics to her as a usurper, and as excommunicated by Papal edict; and their joy in the prospect of her union with the Duke of Anjou, because, although he was a stranger to them, the ties of creed and party were then stronger than all other ties.

Of the Duke himself, he speaks in no flattering terms. "Whether he be not apt to work on the disadvantage of your estate, he is to be judged by his will and power; his will to be as full of light ambition as is possible, beside the French disposition and his own education, his inconstant temper against his brother; his thrusting himself into the Low country matters; his sometimes seeking the King of Spain's daughter, sometimes your Majesty, are evident testimonies of his being carried away with every wind of hope; taught to love greatness any way gotten; and having for the motioners and ministers of the mind only such young men as have shewed they think evil contentment a ground of any rebellion; who have seen no commonwealth but in faction, and divers of which have defiled their hands in odious murders. With such fancies and favorites, what is to be hoped for?"

With pleading earnestness, he portrays the evils that might overwhelm the people under the rule of this turbulent prince; the danger that their interests would be sacrificed to his weakness or ambition; and the folly of presuming upon the amity of the treacherous house of Valois. He alludes to the alliance of her sister Mary with Philip of Spain, the discontent it created in England, and its unhappy effects upon herself; and after speaking of her own "odious marriage with a stranger," he adds: "If your subjects do at this time look for any after-chance, it is but as the pilot doth to the ship boat, if his ship should perish; driven by extremity to the one, but as long as he can with his life, tendering the other."

In a strain of graceful homage, he concludes this spirited epistle: "As for this man, as long as he is but Monsieur in might, and Papist in profession, he neither can nor will greatly shield you; and if he grow to be king, his defence will be like Ajax's shield, which rather weighed down than defended those that bore it. Against contempt, if there be any, which I will never believe, let your excellent virtues of piety, justice, and liberality, daily, if it be possible, more and more shine. Let such particular actions be found out, which be easy as I think to be done, by which you may gratify all the hearts of the people; let those in whom you find trust, and to whom you have committed trust, in your mighty affairs, be held up in the eyes of your subjects; lastly, doing as you do, you shall be, as you be, the example of princes, the ornament of this age, the comfort of the afflicted, the delight of your people, the most excellent fruit of your progenitors, and the perfect mirror of your posterity." *

Philip Sidney had not lived three years at Court without learning that it was no light matter to brave the anger of his "most sweet and gracious sovereign." The vindictiveness which was her inheritance, generally mastered her womanly compassion. Brave and beautiful heads in her reign were laid low upon the scaf-

* Cabala.

fold; high-born hearts pined beneath the frowning battlements of the Tower; and even in the blaze of crackling fagots, rebels sometimes expiated their rebellion. Torture often blanched the lips of the suspected; disgrace and imprisonment were frequent penalties of a hasty retort, or freely expressed opinion. Severe retribution followed the writer, and the printer, of a little book published simultaneously with Sidney's letter. It was entitled, "The discovery of a gaping gulf, wherein England is like to be swallowed by another French marriage, if the Lord forbid not the banns by letting her see the sin and punishment thereof," and these unfortunate men were condemned to lose their right hands. Page, the publisher, exclaimed, as he looked upon his amputated member, "There lies the hand of a true Englishman!" and poor Stubbs, the author, after the axe had fallen upon him, waved his left hand and bravely cried, "God save the Queen!" Probably not one of Elizabeth's ministers would have ventured upon the frank and manly remonstrance which was offered by this fearless young champion. That none of them did so, at least, is certain. Collectively strong, they were, in this matter, individually cautious and irresolute. But Philip Sidney never flinched from duty, and, not even by silence, was traitor to the truth. "The truly valiant," he once said, "dare every thing but to do others an injury." The Queen, irritated with her counsellors and her people, felt, as all others did, the serene ascendency of his pure, exalted mind. The letter was graciously received, the matrimonial negotiations brought to a present pause, and when they were resumed, it was with so much vacillation as to justify the inference that she was playing a political game. The Duke made several efforts to regain his lost ground; but although, in the fascination of his presence, the royal maiden faltered as any rustic maiden of her realm might have done beneath the gaze of Corydon or Damon, and although, as the chroniclers tell us, she wore a gold ornament in which his "phisnomye" was painted, and gave him in public a ring from her own finger, besides many unmistakable evidences of affection, yet we may well believe that this pungent appeal haunted her memory, and prompted her final resolve.

Sidney maintained a constant correspondence with his venerable friend Languet, keeping him apprized of all his movements, and gratefully receiving his paternal counsels. After this letter to the Queen became publicly known, Languet expressed much apprehension lest the French should seek personal revenge upon the writer, and he warns him to be upon his guard, if the Duke of Anjou should visit England with a large retinue. But Sir Fulke Greville says: "He kept access to her Majesty as before, and a liberal conversation among the French, reverenced amongst the worthiest of them for himself, and born in too strong a fortification of nature for the less worthy to treat either with question, familiarity, or scorn."

In truth, the only enemy that Sidney seems to have had was the Earl of Oxford, a weak, wicked man, and the veriest coxcomb in the kingdom. He had no distinction but that of having first introduced into England perfumed and embroidered gloves from Spain. He presented the Queen with a pair, decorated with tufts of rose-colored silk, which she always wore when she sat for her portraits. After this time, he further distinguished himself by ruining his fortune, defacing his beautiful castles, and pre-determinately breaking the heart of his wife,* in revenge upon her father, Lord Burleigh, because he refused to interfere in behalf of the Duke of Norfolk, of

* While Sidney was a student at Oxford, a treaty of marriage was proposed between this lady and himself. Lord Burleigh and Sir Henry held some correspondence on the subject, and it does not seem to be known why the negotiations were not concluded.

whom the Earl was a special friend. He was, at this time, the head of the French faction; and, doubtless, provoked at the part which Sidney had taken in the proposed alliance. So, one day, when the latter was playing his favorite game of tennis, the Earl entered the tennis court, and insolently ordered him to leave it. This Sidney of course refused to do; whereupon the Earl, with added wrath, repeated the command, calling him, among other abusive epithets, a *puppy*. A crowd of noblemen and courtiers were by this time gathered; the French legation with the rest. Perhaps Philip Sidney should have scorned "to stain the temper of his knightly sword" with foeman so unworthy, but he answered the insult by a haughty challenge. Oxford sullenly refused either an acceptance or an apology. Sidney repeated his defiance, and the quarrel waxed fierce. The lords of the privy council vainly attempted to mediate, and at last the Queen interposed. Sending for Sidney, she told him that "there was a great difference in degree between earls and private gentlemen, and that princes were born to support the nobility, and to insist on their being treated with proper respect." His was not the spirit to quail at the undeserved rebuke of even sceptred power. With becoming respect, but fearless independence, he adroitly refuted the argument. "That place," he said, "was never intended for privilege to wrong; witness herself, who, soever sovereign she were by throne, birth, education and nature, yet was she content to cast her own affections into the same mould her subjects did, and govern all her rights by the laws. And although the Earl was a great lord by birth, alliance, and grace, yet he was no lord over him; and therefore the difference between free men could not challenge any other homage than precedency." He then reminds her that her father "gave the gentry free and safe appeal against the opinions of the grandees, and found it wisdom by the stronger combination of numbers, to keep down the greater power." *

This was bold trenching upon royal ground. We do not hear of another youth, gentleman or peer, who could with impunity have led Majesty to the well and shown her Truth at the bottom. But it was all taken in good part, and perhaps Elizabeth was even pleased with the intrepid spirit of her knight.

This affair was, doubtless, annoying to his sensitive mind; and, besides, he was tired of the monotony of court life. He wrote a year previously to Languet, that he earnestly desired pri-

* Fulke Greville's Life of Sir Philip Sidney.

vacy and leisure. Soon after this, he asked leave from the Queen to pass some time at Wilton, the residence of his sister, the Countess of Pembroke. During this visit, he wrote his first work; a famous romance, called the *Arcadia.* A richly carved oak chair, which he usually occupied in the library at Wilton, is even now preserved as a precious relic; and visitors are still admitted to another room there, the panels of which represent the shepherds and the knights, the rustic dances and the martial deeds, of Sidney's story.

CHAPTER VII.

THE Arcadia of Sir Philip Sidney is a mixture of the old Gothic romance with the Italian pastoral. As it was one of the standard works of that century, and is still venerated as a literary curiosity, let us take down from its shelf a rare old copy printed in 1638, and cull therefrom a few specimen passages, weaving them together with a brief outline of the story.

The work opens with a dialogue between two shepherds, idly stretched upon a sandy beach of Laconia, on the charms of a certain damsel, of whom they declare that "as the greatest thing in the world is her beauty, so that is the least thing that may be praised in her." They are diverted from the theme by the sudden appearance of a man, floating on the fragment of a shattered vessel. As soon as their care has restored his senses, he begs them to seek for his friend Pyrocles, who is also a victim of the wreck. Engaging the services of some fishermen, they proceed in the search, accompanied by the stranger, Musidorus, who promises to reward them from a casket of jewels, which he has managed to save. They soon espy, seated upon the broken mast, a youth of wondrous beauty, scantily apparelled in a garment wrought with blue silk and gold, and waving a sword with defiant air above his head. The simple fishermen imagine him some god of the sea, but Musidorus, with joyful recognition of his friend, assures them that "he is but a man, although of divine excellencies." But now heaves in sight a pirate ship, well known to them as a cruiser for slaves for the galleys, and the terrified mariners ply their boat hastily homeward, leaving poor Pyrocles,—embroidered toga, sword, and all,—in hopeless solitude. Musidorus is in despair, knowing what is now the inevitable fate of his comrade. The shepherds, compassionating his grief, advise him to seek the protection of a fine old Arcadian gentleman, named Kalander; "a man who for his hospitality is so much haunted that no news stirs but comes to his ears; for his upright dealing so beloved of his neighbors, that he hath many ever ready to do him their uttermost service; to him we will bring you, and there you may recover your health, without which you will not be able to make any diligent search for your friend." With comforting care, they conduct him to Arcadia, arriving there "in the time that the morning did strew roses and violets in the heavenly floor, against the coming of the sun." Here follows one of the poetical descriptions with which the book abounds: "There were hills which garnished their proud heights with stately trees; humble valleys whose base estate seemed comforted with the refreshing of silver rivers; meadows enamelled with all sorts of eye-pleasing flowers; thickets which being lined with most pleasant shade, were witnessed so, too, by the cheerful disposition of many well-tuned birds; each pasture stored with sheep, feeding with sober security, while the pretty lambs with bleating oratory craved the dam's comfort; here a shepherd's boy, piping as though he should never be old; there a young shepherdess, knitting, and withal singing, and it seemed that her voice comforted her hands to work, and her hands kept time to her voice music."—"A happy people," he says, "were the Arcadians; wanting little, because they desired not much." The house of Kalander he pleasantly describes as "built of fair and shewy stone, not affecting so much any extravagant kind of fineness, as an honorable representing of a firm stateliness. The lights, doors, and stairs, rather directed to the use of the guest than to the eye of the artificer."—"All more lasting than beautiful, but that the consideration of the exceeding lastingness made the eye believe it was exceeding beautiful. The servants, not so many in number as cleanly in apparel and serviceable in behavior, testifying even in their countenances that their master took as well care to be served as of them that did serve."* The worthy host receives Musidorus with great hospitality, nurses him through a long illness, and sends out a galley in search of Pyrocles; and finding in his guest "a mind of most excellent composition, a piercing wit quite devoid of ostentation, high-erected thoughts seated in a heart of courtesy, an eloquence as sweet in the uttering as slow to come to the uttering, a behavior so noble as gave a majesty to adversity, and all in a man whose age could not be above one and twenty years, the good old man was even enamored with a fatherly love toward him."

Among various objects of taste in this Arcadian home, such as gardens, statues, and pictures, Musidorus is one day attracted by the portraits of a "comely old man, a lady of middle age but of excellent beauty," and a maiden of surpassing loveliness. Kalander explains that they represent

* It is thought that this description was intended as a picture of Penshurst Castle, Sir Philip's early home.

the royal family of Arcadia; and proceeds to say that Basilius the King, having received an unpleasant prophecy from the Delphian oracle, had determined to avert its fulfilment by breaking up his court, and burying himself, and his wife and daughters, in the solitude of a forest hard by. He describes Basilius as "not exceeding in the virtues which get admiration, as depth of wisdom, height of courage, and largeness of magnificence, but notable in those which stir affection, as truth of word, meekness, courtesy, mercifulness, and liberality." Gynecia, his wife, many years younger than himself, is "a woman of great wit, and more princely virtues than her husband; of so working a mind and so vehement spirits, as a man may say, it was happy she took a good course, for otherwise it would have been terrible." Of the daughters he says, "there is more sweetness in Philoclea, more majesty in Pamela; methought love played in Philoclea's eye, and threatened in Pamela's; Philoclea's beauty only persuaded, but so as hearts must yield,—Pamela's used violence, as no hearts could resist." Philoclea is humble and diffident, Pamela full of wise and lofty thought.

Some days after, Musidorus discovers that Kalander has heard some painful news which he conceals from his guest, because the laws of hospitality, "long and holily observed by him, give such a sway to his proceedings that he will in no way suffer the stranger lodged under his roof to receive any infection of his anguish." Musidorus hears from the steward of the household that Clitophon, Kalander's only son, having gone off on a chivalrous service for a friend, had become accidentally engaged in a battle between the Helots and their masters, and was a prisoner in the hands of the former. Musidorus resolves to attempt the rescue of Clitophon; and Kalander, with joyful assent, assembling two hundred Arcadian gentlemen, they enter the Helot camp by stratagem. After a sharp conflict, in which the Arcadians lose ground, Musidorus proposes to decide the day by single combat with the Helot captain. "And so they began a fight which was so much inferior to the battle in noise and number as it was surpassing it in bravery, and, as it were, delightful terribleness. Their courage was guided with skill, and their skill was armed with courage; neither did their hardness darken their wit, nor their wit cool their hardness; both valiant, as men despising death; both confident, as unwonted to be overcome,—their feet steady, their hands diligent, their eyes watchful, and their hearts resolute."

Musidorus at last receives a blow which knocks

off his helmet, and, reeling backward, is astonished to see his foe kneeling at his feet, and offering him the hilt of his sword, in token of submission. It is his lost friend Pyrocles, who has just discovered with whom he is contending. Matters are soon amicably adjusted between the belligerent parties; Clitophon is released, and the two friends return home with Kalander.

After a few days of social enjoyment, Musidorus perceives that Pyrocles is silent and abstracted, seeking solitude in the woods and gardens "as if his only comfort was to be without a comforter." Attributing this sadness to long absence from their home in Thessaly, where they both held the rank of princes, he proposes that they return thither. Receiving no encouragement, he proceeds to reason with him upon the change in his conduct.

"A mind well trained and long exercised in virtue, doth not easily change any course it once undertakes, but upon well-grounded and well-weighed causes, but whereas you were wont to give yourself vehemently to the knowledge of those things which might better your mind, to seek the familiarity of excellent men in soldiery and learning, and to put all these things in practice, you now leave them all undone; you let your mind fall asleep; beside your countenance troubled, which surely comes not of virtue; for virtue, like the clear heaven, is without clouds; and lastly, you subject yourself to solitariness, the sly enemy that doth most separate a man from well-doing."

Pyrocles, after acknowledging the kindness of the expostulation, defends himself by saying, "These knowledges, as they are of good use, yet are they not all the mind may stretch itself unto; who knows whether I feed not my mind with higher thoughts? Truly, though I know not all the particularities, yet I see the bounds of all these knowledges; but the workings of the mind I find much more infinite. And in such contemplation I enjoy my solitariness; and my solitariness, perchance, is the nurse of these contemplations. Eagles we see fly alone, and they are but sheep which always herd together.—And doth not the pleasantness of this place carry in it sufficient reward for any time lost in it? Do you not see how all things conspire to make this country a heavenly dwelling? Do you not see the grasses, how in color they excel the emeralds, each one striving to pass his fellow, and yet they are all kept of equal height? Do not these stately trees seem to maintain their flourishing old age, with the happiness of their seat, being clothed with a continual spring, because no beauty here should ever fade? Doth not the air breathe health, which the birds, delightful both to eye and ear, do daily solemnize with the sweet consent of their voices? And these fresh and delightful brooks, how slowly they glide away, as loth to leave the company of so many united things in perfection; and with how sweet a murmur they lament the forced departure. Certainly it must be that some goddess inhabiteth this region who is the soul of this soil."

Musidorus is not quite satisfied with this adroit subterfuge; but the conversation is interrupted by Kalander, who comes to invite their presence at a stag hunt. After the hunt, Pyrocles is missing, and a letter to Musidorus informs him that his friend is the hopeless victim of the tender passion. He is much disturbed by the flight of Pyrocles, and again starts in search of him, to the grief of Kalander, who, however, "knowing it to be more cumber than courtesy to strive, abstains from urging him."

After two months of unrewarded knight-errantry, in the course of which he meets with various remarkable adventures, he returns despondingly to Arcadia. One day, while reposing under the shade of a forest-tree, he is surprised by the sight of a beautiful Amazon, clad in a doublet of blue satin, decked with gold plates in imitation of mail, crimson velvet buskins, on her head a coronet of gold and feathers made to resemble a helmet, and at her side a sword. Entering an arbor "of trees with branches lovingly interlaced," and singing a doleful love-ditty, her features reveal to the astonished Musidorus his long-sought Pyrocles. Grieved at this unmanly disguise, he addresses him in a strain of affectionate reproof; reminds him of his noble birth, and that he is now forfeiting the fame with which his previous life had been rewarded; "as if you should drown your ship in the desired haven, or as if an ill player should mar the last act of his tragedy." "Remember, that if we will be men, the reasonable part of our soul is to have absolute commandment."—"Nay, we are to resolve that if reason direct it, we must do it; and if we must do it, we will do it." With impatient vehemence, he denounces, in a tirade worthy of the great Cynic himself, the passion that has been "the author of all these troubles"—"it is nothing but a certain base weakness, which some fools call a gentle heart; his companions are unquiet longings, fond comforts, faint discomforts, hopes, jealousies, ungrounded rages, causeless yieldings; so is the highest end it aspires unto, a little pleasure, with much pain before, and great repentance after. It truly subverts the course of nature, making reason give place to sense, and man to woman." "True love," he adds, "hath that excellent nature in it, that it doth transform the very essence of the lover into the thing loved; uniting, and as it were, incorporating it with a secret and inward working. The love of heaven makes one heavenly; the love of virtue, virtuous; but this effeminate love of a woman doth so womanize a man that if he yield to it, it will not only make an Amazon, but a launder, a distaff, a spinner, or whatsoever vile occupation his idle head can imagine, and his weak hands perform. Therefore if either you remember what you are, what you have been, or what you must be; if you consider by what kind of creature you are moved, you shall find the cause so small, the effect so dangerous, and both so unworthy of you, that I doubt not I shall quickly have occasion rather to praise you for having conquered it, than to give you farther counsel how to do it." Pyrocles, though displeased with this expostulation, pardons it "from the exceeding good-will he bears to Musidorus." He takes up the cudgels in behalf of the despised sex, and reminds him that if men have such excellence, it is reasonable to attribute it, in part at least, to their mothers, "since a kite never brought forth a good flying hawk." The invective against love, he says, should be levelled against him, rather than against love itself; "above all, not against that divine creature who hath joined me and love together," and avows, that notwithstanding his womanly attire, he will prove himself a man in that enterprise. After much sharp shooting on both sides, Musidorus indignantly exclaims, "I now beseech you, even for the love betwixt us, (if this other love hath left any in you towards me,) for the remembrance of your father, and for your own sake, to purge yourself of this vile infection; otherwise give me leave to leave off this name of friendship, as an idle title of a thing which cannot be where virtue is not established." In the accents of wounded affection Pyrocles replies, "Alas, how cruelly you deal with me; if you seek the victory, take it; and if ye list, the triumph; have you all the reason of the world, and with me remain all the imperfections; yet such as I can no more lay from me than the Crow can be persuaded by the Swan to cast off his black feathers. But truly you deal with me like a physician, that seeing his patient in a pestilent fever, should chide him, instead of ministering help, and bid him be sick no more; or rather like such a friend, that visiting his friend condemned to perpetual prison and laden with grievous fetters, should will him to shake off his fetters or he would leave him. I am sick, and sick to the death; I am prisoner, neither is there any redress but by her to whom I am a slave. Now, if you list, leave him that loves you in the highest degree. But remember ever to carry this with you, that you abandon your friend in his greatest extremity." "And herewith the deep wound of his love being rubbed afresh with this new unkindness, began as it were to bleed again, in such a sort as he was unable to bear it any longer, but gushing out abundance of tears, and crossing his arms over his woful heart, he sunk down to the ground; which sudden trance went so to the heart of Musidorus, that, falling down by him and kissing the weeping eyes of his friend, he besought him not to make account of his speech; which, if it had been over vehement, yet was it to be borne withal, because it came out of a love much more vehement; but now, finding in him the force of it, he would no farther contrary it, but employ all his service to medicine it. But even this kindness made Pyrocles the more to melt in the former unkindness, which his manlike tears well showed, with a silent look upon Musidorus, as who should say, and is it possible that Musidorus should threaten to leave me? And this struck Musidorus's mind and senses so dumb too, that, for grief, not being able to say any thing, they rested with their eyes placed one upon another in such sort as well might point out the true passion of unkindness to be never aright but betwixt them that dearly love." *

A complete reconciliation ensues, and Musidorus begs to hear the story of Pyrocles's misfortunes, because "between friends all must be told, nothing being superfluous or tedious." "Assure yourself," he says, "there is nothing so great which I will fear to do for you, and nothing so

* D'Israeli has remarked, in allusion probably to this dialogue, "There is something in the language and the conduct of Musidorus and Pyrocles, which may startle the reader, and may be condemned as very unnatural and most affected. Their friendship resembles the love which is felt for the beautiful sex, if we were to decide by their impassioned conduct, and the tenderness of their language. Coleridge observed that the language of these two friends in the Arcadia is such as we would not now use, except to women; and he has thrown out some very remarkable observations. . . . It is unquestionably a remains of the ancient chivalry, when men, embarking in the same perilous enterprise together, vowed their mutual aid and their personal devotion. The dangers of one knight were to be participated, and his honor to be maintained, by his brother-in-arms. Such exalted friendships, and such interminable affections, often broke out both in deeds and words which, to the tempered intercourse of our day, offend by their intensity."—*Amenities of Literature*, vol. 2.

small which I will disdain to do." Pyrocles proceeds to explain that when he first saw in Kalander's house the portrait of Philoclea, he "quickly received a cruel impression of that wonderful passion which to be defined is impossible, because no words reach to the strange nature of it; they only know it who inwardly feel it; it is called Love." All that he saw and heard seemed but to feed the flame, although he calls to witness "the eternal spring of virtue," that he summoned all reason and philosophy to his aid. "Nothing in truth could hold any plea with it, but the reverent friendship I bear unto you, feeling that there is nothing more terrible to a guilty heart than the eye of a respected friend." Hearing from Kalander that Basilius was obstinately bent on keeping his daughters from matrimony, in consequence of the warning of the oracle, he had determined to obtain admission to the presence of his fair one, in the disguise of an Amazon.. Basilius, finding him alone in the forest near the royal dwelling, and smitten with the beauty of the supposed lady, marvelled at her solitude. "They are never alone," he replied, "that are accompanied by noble thoughts." Pyrocles passed himself off as the niece of the Amazonian Queen, shipwrecked on that coast, and had ingratiated himself with the royal family even more successfully than he desired. He enjoyed the society of Philoclea, who, not suspecting his sex, was yet conscious of strange heart flutterings in his presence; but the old king had conceived a violent passion for the beautiful Amazon, which he displayed by pertinacious attention; and, to crown the ludicrous entanglement of the knight, Gynecia, the queen, had seen through his disguise, and become deeply enamored of him. Between the plots and counterplots which this precious pair contrived for the purpose of deceiving each other and securing their own aim, Pyrocles had had a very thorny time to preserve his own dignity, and secure the love of Philoclea.

At this crisis, Musidorus is added to the *dramatis personæ*, and being introduced to them as an Arcadian shepherd, he is unsuspectingly received into the service of Basilius. Pyrocles is soon avenged for the past rebukes of the woman-hating Musidorus, by finding that he, too, soon takes to solitary rambles and melancholy plaints, and hears with malicious pleasure that he is ensnared by the fair Pamela. "I find indeed,' says the penitent type of myriad successors "that all is but lip wisdom which wants experience. Well do I see that Love, to a yielding heart, is a king; but to a resisting one, a tyrant."

Meanwhile the sisters are not insensible to the attractions of the young princes, who in due time reveal to them their incognito. The latter tell the story of their past lives, and describe, in one of the fine passages of that nature with which the book abounds, the shipwreck that threw them on the coast of Greece. "There arose even with the sun a veil of black clouds before his face, which shortly, like ink poured into water, had blacked all over the face of heaven; preparing, as it were, a mournful stage for a tragedy to be played on. For forthwith the winds began to speak louder, and, as in a tumultuous kingdom, to think themselves fittest instruments of commandment; and blowing whole storms of hail and rain upon them, they were sooner in danger than they could almost bethink themselves of change. For then the traitorous sea began to swell in pride against the afflicted navy, under which, while the heaven favored them, it had lain so calmly; making mountains of itself, over which the tossed and tottering ship should climb, to be straight carried down again to a pit of hellish darkness, with such cruel blows against the side of the ship, that, which way soever it went, was still in his malice, that there was neither left power to stay nor way to escape. And shortly had it so dissevered the loving company, which the day before had tarried together, that most of them never met again, but were swallowed up in his never-satisfied mouth. There was to be seen the diverse manner of minds in distress; some sat upon the top of the poop, weeping and wailing till the sea swallowed them; some one more able to abide death, than fear of death, cut his own throat to prevent drowning; some prayed; and there wanted not of them which cursed, as if the heavens could not be more angry than they were." An incident which they witnessed in the course of their adventures, is supposed to have suggested to Shakspeare the story of Gloster, in King Lear. Overtaken by a violent storm, they had taken refuge within a hollow rock, and were auditors of a conversation between a blind old man and a youth who was leading him; "both poorly arrayed and extremely weather-beaten, yet in both there seemed a kind of nobleness not suitable to that affliction." The elder proved to be the king of Paphlagonia, deprived of his kingdom and his sight by a bastard son; and, attended in his banishment by a dutiful, but unloved, legitimate child, he had by coaxing and entreaty made his way to the summit of this high rock, with the purpose of ending his misfortunes by a headlong leap.

Philoclea is overwhelmed with delight to find that her Zelmane is no other than the Prince

Pyrocles, whose fame had often reached her—"such joy as wrought into Pygmalion's mind, when he found his beloved image was softer and warmer in his folded arms, till at length it accomplished his gladness with a perfect woman's shape. Yet doubt would fain have played his part in her mind, and called in question how she should be assured that Zelmane was Pyrocles. But love stood straight up and deposed that a lie could not come from the mouth of Zelmane. With sweet timidity she confesses the story of her faith, and says, 'Thou hast then the victory—use it with virtue. Dost thou love me? Keep me then still worthy to be loved.'"

Numerous pastoral sports and whimsical feats of arms "give feathers to the wings of time," as Sidney says; but, however entertaining to Arcadian lovers and those of his own day, modern taste has so far outrun their quaint insipidity, that we refrain from quotation.

After several weeks' interval, during which the king and queen ingeniously torture themselves and every body else, and the knights maintain their constancy and honor, a checkmate is threatened from a new quarter. Cecropia, Queen of Argos, and aunt of the princesses, incensed that the marriage overtures of her son Amphialus to Philoclea have been refused, and his succession thus lost to the throne of Arcadia, contrives a plan to secure the possession of both. So one day while the princesses and the pretended Amazon are regaling themselves with grapes and plums in the forest, they are all seized by a party of armed men and forcibly carried to a fortified castle, built upon a high rock in the midst of a lake. Here they are closely confined in separate apartments, "wanting nothing but liberty and comfort," and not permitted to see or hear from each other. Cecropia's object is to compel, by either persuasion or force, one of the sisters to marry her son; and Basilius, she argues, will soon die from grief at their loss. Amphialus, who is "an excellent son of an evil mother, like a rose out of a briar," disapproves the stratagem, but accepts it as an occasion to plead his cause with Philoclea, of whom he is deeply enamored. Arraying himself in black velvet embroidered with pearl, and a broad collar of diamonds, rubies, and opals, set in white enamel, he betakes himself to her chamber. The gentle damsel was in very disconsolate mood, but "in the book of her beauty there was nothing to be read but sorrow; for kindness was blotted out and anger was never there." He pleads his cause with much waste of eloquence, avowing that her face is his astronomy, her goodness, his philosophy; to which he receives the frigid assurance that she will find a way to death rather than accept him. Cecropia, incensed at her obstinacy, and grieved by the despair of her son, tries her own persuasive power, masking her malice under a loving mien. She begins the attack by an artful appeal to her feminine vanity: "Fie upon this peevish sadness! Look upon your own body, and see whether it deserve to pine away with sorrow! see whether you will have these hands fade from their whiteness and softness, and become dry, lean, and yellow; and make everybody wonder at the change, and say, that sure you had used some art before, for if the beauties had been natural they would never so soon have been blemished. Take a glass, and see whether tears become your eyes; although I confess those eyes are able to make tears comely." "Alas!" answers Philoclea, "I know not whether tears become my eyes, but I am sure that my eyes, thus beteared, become my fortune." Finding this tack unsuccessful, Cecropia tries another. She pictures the charms of married life, and says that she has come to offer her their "true and essential happiness." "Have you ever seen a pure rose-water kept in a crystal glass? how fine it looks, how sweet it smells, while that beautiful glass imprisons it? Break the prison, and let the water take its own course: doth it not embrace dust, and lose all its former sweetness and fairness? Truly so are we, if we have not the stay rather than the restraint of crystalline marriage. My heart melts to think of the sweet comforts I in that time received, when I had never cause to care, but the care was doubled; when I never rejoiced, but that I saw my joy shine in another's eyes. What shall I say of the free delight which the heart might embrace, without the accusing of the inward conscience, or the fear of outward shame? And is a solitary life as good as this? Then can one string make as good music as a concert; then can one color set forth a beauty."

Mother and son are equally unsuccessful; Philoclea pines for her captive lover; is unmoved by the splendid gifts daily sent to her by Amphialus, and heedless of the delightful music that is nightly poured forth beneath her window. As the one sister continues intractable, Cecropia points her batteries upon the other, hoping that Amphialus will turn his affections into the successful channel. She proceeds to Pamela's chamber, and hearing her voice, pauses to listen. The high-minded maiden, resolutely fortifying herself against present and feared calamity, paces the floor "with deep and patient thought," and gives utterance to her emotion in this beautiful invocation:—

"O All-seeing Light, and eternal Life of all

things! to whom nothing is either so great that it may resist, or so small that it is contemned; look upon my misery with thine eye of mercy, and let thine infinite power vouchsafe to limit out some proportion of deliverance unto me, as to thee shall seem most convenient. Let not injury, O Lord, triumph over me, and let my faults by thy hand be corrected, and make not mine unjust enemy the minister of thy justice. But yet, my God, if in thy wisdom this be the aptest chastisement for my inexcusable folly; if this low bondage be fittest for my over-high desires; if the pride of my not enough humble heart be not enough to be broken, O Lord, I yield unto thy will, and joyfully embrace what sorrow thou wilt have me suffer. Only thus much let me crave of thee, (let my craving, O Lord, be accepted of thee, since even that proceeds from thee,) let me crave even by the noblest title, which in my greatest affliction I may give myself, that I am thy creature, and by thy goodness (which is thyself) that thou wilt suffer some beam of thy majesty so to shine into my mind, that it may still depend confidently on thee. Let calamity be the exercise, but not the overthrow, of my virtue; let their power prevail, but prevail not to destruction; let my greatness be their prey; let my pain be the sweetness of their revenge; let them (if so it seem good unto thee) vex me with more and more punishment. But, O Lord, let never their wickedness have such a hand but that I may carry a pure mind in a pure body!"* And pausing awhile—"and, O most gracious Lord," said she, "whatever becomes of me, preserve the virtuous Musidorus."

As may be supposed, Cecropia found herself again foiled, for if "Philoclea with sweet and humble dealing did avoid her assaults, Pamela with the majesty of virtue beat them off."

Amphialus and his mother are diverted, for a time, by an attack upon the castle, from the partizans of Basilius. The assailants are driven back, after a good display of bravery on both sides, and "no sword pays so large a tribute of souls to the eternal kingdom as that of Amphialus." One knight, who has hitherto been of those who "fight and run away," loses his head, and, in his dying convulsions, forcing his spurs into his steed, the animal rushes so madly into the enemy's ranks as

* This prayer is celebrated as having been often repeated by Charles I. during his imprisonment; and he held in his hand, as he ascended the scaffold, the Eikon Basilikae, in which a copy of it was included. Milton pours upon him a vial of puritanical wrath for using a petition "addressed by a heathen woman to a heathen god," and quoted from the "vain amatorious poem" of the Arcadia. However, as he also censures the monarch for *plagiarizing* passages from David's Psalms, the arrow against Sir Philip falls harmless.

to occasion the proverb that "Policrates was only valiant after his head was cut off." A more poetical end is that of Phebilus, who, "having long loved Philoclea, though for the meanness of his estate he durst not reveal it," is attacked by Amphialus, when, "thinking to die, he cries, 'O Philoclea! this joys me that I die for thy sake!'" His antagonist, hearing this, will not vouchsafe him the honor of dying for Philoclea, but turns his sword another way, "doing him no hurt for over much hatred. But what good did that to poor Phebilus, if, escaping a valiant hand, he was slain by a base soldier, who, seeing him so disarmed, thrust him through?"

The alarm being dispelled, Cecropia renews her attack upon the captive sisters. From Philoclea she receives no answer "but a silence sealed up in virtue, and so sweetly graced as that in one instant it carries with it both grace and humbleness." "Pamela, having wearied herself with reading, and disdaining the company of the gentlewomen appointed to attend her, was working upon a purse certain roses and lilies. The flowers she had wrought carried such life in them that the cunningest painter might have learned of her needle; which, with so pretty a manner, made his careers to and fro the cloth, as if the needle itself would have been loth to go from such a mistress, but that it hoped to return thitherward very quickly again; the cloth looking with many eyes upon her and lovingly embracing the wounds she gave it; the shears also were at hand to behead the silk that was grown too short. "Full happy is he," begins the artful Cecropia, "to whom a purse, by this manner and by this hand wrought, is dedicated. In faith he shall have cause to account it not as a purse for treasure, but as a treasure in itself." "I promise you," says Pamela, "I wrought it but to make tedious hours believe I thought not of them." The beauty of the purse furnishes Cecropia a text to descant upon that of Pamela. She dwells in glowing language upon her charms, reminds her of her father's determination to keep aloof all admirers, and asks, "Will you suffer your beauty to be hidden in the wrinkles of his peevish thoughts?" "If he be peevish," replied Pamela, "yet is he my father; and how beautiful soever I be, I am his daughter; God claims at my hand obedience, and makes me no judge of his imperfections." Cecropia now thinks that if this conscientious maiden can be made to doubt the overruling Deity in whom she believes, her scruples may be overcome; and she proceeds to attack her faith with the arguments that we still hear from bewildered mystics and freethinkers. "Foolish fear and ignorance were the first inventers of those conceits. Chance is the only cause of all things—yesterday was but as to-day; and to-morrow will tread the same footsteps as his foregoers; so as is manifest enough that all things follow but the course of its own nature, saving only man, who, while by the pregnancy of his imagination he strives to things supernatural, meanwhile he loseth his own natural felicity. Be wise, and that wisdom shall be a god unto thee; be contented, and that is thy heaven; for to think that those powers, if there be any such, are moved either by the eloquence of our prayers, or in a chafe at the folly of our actions, carries as much reason as if flies should think, that men take great care which of them hums sweetest, and which of them flies nimblest."

Pamela's indignant reply is the still unanswerable refutation of atheism; and so forcible and clear that it is all well worth transcribing, but we can quote only a few passages:—

"Peace, peace! unworthy to breathe, that dost not acknowledge the breath-giver! most unworthy to have a tongue, which speakest against Him through whom thou speakest! you say, yesterday was as to-day. What doth that argue but that there is a constancy in the everlasting Governor? Would you have an inconstant God? since we count a man foolish that is inconstant. He is not seen, you say, and yet you might see enough of the Creator in his works, if you were not like such who for sport-sake willingly hoodwink themselves, to receive blows the easier. You say because we know not the causes of things, therefore fear was the mother of superstition; nay, because we know that each effect hath a cause, *that* hath engendered a true and lively devotion. Do we not see goodly cause for this lively faith in all around? For this lovely world of which we are, and in which we live, hath not its being by chance; on which opinion of chance, it is beyond marvel by what chance any brain could stumble. For if it be eternal, as you would seem to conceive it, eternity and chance are things unsufferable together; for that is chanceable which happeneth; and if it happen, there was a time before it happened when it might not have happened; or else it did not happen; and so, if chanceable, not eternal; and if eternal, not of chance. And as absurd it is to think that if it had a beginning, its beginning was derived from chance; for chance could never make all things of nothing; and if there were substances before, which by chance should meet to make up this world, thereon follows another bottomless pit of absurdities; for then those substances must needs have been from ever, and so eternal; and that eternal causes should bring forth chanceable effects, is as sensible as that the sun should be the author of darkness. Again, if it were chanceable, then was it not necessary; whereby you take away all consequents. But we see in all things, in some respect or other, necessity of consequence; therefore in reason we must know that causes were necessary. Besides, chance is variable, or else it is not to be called chance; but we see this world is steady and permanent. If nothing but chance had glued these pieces of this all, the heavy parts would have gone infinitely downwards, the light infinitely upward, and so never have met to have made up this goodly body. Perfect order, perfect beauty, perfect constancy, if these be the children of chance, let wisdom be counted the root of wickedness! But you may perhaps affirm, that one universal nature is the knitting together of these many parts, to such an excellent unity. If you mean a nature of wisdom, goodness, and providence, which knows what it doth, then say you that which I seek of you; but if you mean a nature as we speak of the fire, which goeth upward it knows not why, and of the nature of the sea, which in ebbing and flowing, seems to observe so just a dance, and yet understands no music: it is still but the same absurdity, superscribed with another title. This world cannot otherwise consist, but by a mind of wisdom, which governs it; which, whether you will allow to be the Creator thereof, as undoubtedly he is, or the soul and Governor thereof;—most certain it is, that whether he govern all, or make all, his power is above either his creatures or his government. And if his power be above all things, then, consequently, it must needs be infinite, since there is nothing above it to limit it. For, beyond which there is nothing, must needs be boundless and infinite. If his power be infinite, then likewise must his knowledge be infinite. If his knowledge and power be infinite, then must needs his goodness and justice march in the same rank; for infiniteness of power and knowledge, without like measure of goodness must necessarily bring forth destruction and ruin, and not ornament and preservation. Since, then, there is a God, and an all-knowing God, so as he seeth into the darkest of all natural secrets, which is the heart of man; and sees therein the deepest dissembled thoughts; nay, sees the thoughts before they be thought;—since he is just, to exercise his might; and mighty to perform his justice; assure thyself that the time will come, when thou shalt know that power, by feeling it; when thou shalt see his wisdom, in the manifesting thy shamefulness; and shalt only perceive him to have been a Creator in thy destruction"!

"And here," says Sidney, "Cecropia, like a bat, (which, though it have eyes to discern the sun, yet hath so evil eyes that it cannot delight in the sun,) found a truth, but could not love it."

The story of the beleaguered princesses having spread through Greece, many renowned paladins came to their rescue, and for a long time we hear only the trumpet of victory, and see the glittering armor and pawing steeds of the battle-field. One knight rides a milk-white charger, whose mane and tail are dyed crimson, his caparison is an imitation of vine-branches, and hung with clusters of grapes; the rider is in blue armor; on his shield is a grayhound outrunning his fellows, and the motto, "The glory, not the prey." Of another, named Argalus, there is a pretty story told, which we will epitomize, as illustrative of the character of Sir Philip's favorite heroes. He is about to marry the beautiful Parthenia, when a discarded rival, incensed with his own refusal, forms a fiendish plot to avenge himself, and punish the lovers. Obtaining an interview with Parthenia, under the mask of friendship, he forcibly seizes her, and rubs upon her face a virulent poison, which occasions a long illness, and utterly destroys her beauty. Argalus, who had gone away to invite his wedding guests, returns home with joyful expectancy, only to find his bride in this lamentable state, and heroically resolved to release him from his vows. In vain he protests against the Iphigenian sacrifice, and declares that his love is but deepened by her misfortunes. Parthenia long resists his importunity, and finally quits the country without leaving any clue to her wanderings. In the bitterness of despair, Argalus starts off on a crusade against his rival, who had enlisted in the war of the Helots, and in the course of his migrations becomes a guest of Kalander, at the same time with Pyrocles and Musidorus. One day, as they are all discoursing together in the banqueting hall, Argalus is told that a young and noble lady desires an audience with him. With amazed delight he beholds, as he supposes, his lost Parthenia, restored to all her native loveliness; but the lady, with grave dignity of mien, tells him that he is mistaken; she is a niece of Helen, Queen of Corinth, and a cousin of Parthenia, whom she nearly resembles. "Parthenia," she says, "sought refuge in Corinth, and died a few days since, leaving for Argalus a message which she had promised to deliver." With modest grace, the damsel communicates Parthenia's request, that Argalus would receive and espouse this friend, whose character and person are so similar to her own, that she cannot fail to prove an acceptable substitute. Argalus thanks her for a proffer so complimentary, and avows himself ready to fulfil all her behests as her slave through life; that if his heart were his to give, she should have that too; but it was in the grave of Parthenia, and he felt that he should not long tarry after her. "If it were only her beauty that I love," he says, "I should love you who have the same beauty; but it was Parthenia's self, with a love which no likeness can make, no commandment dissolve, no foulness defile, and no death finish." The veritable Parthenia, who has been cured by the Queen's physician, and has tested by this stratagem the constancy of her lover, now confesses her identity; the nuptials are celebrated, and Kalander, with his other guests, unites in them with friendly zeal. After the daughters of Basilius are carried off to the old fortress by the lake, he sends a request to his kinsman, Argalus, to challenge Amphialus for their rescue. Here follows an exquisite little picture of married bliss:—

"The messenger made haste, and found Argalus at a castle of his own, sitting in a parlor with the fair Parthenia, he reading aloud the stories of Hercules, she by him, as to hear him read; but while his eyes looked on the book, she ıooked on his eyes, sometimes staying him with some pretty question, not so much to be resolved of the doubt, as to give him occasion to look upon her. A happy couple, he joying in her, she joying in herself, because she enjoyed him; both increased their riches by giving to each other, each making one life double, because they made a double life one, where desire never wanted satisfaction, nor satisfaction ever bred satiety; he ruling, because she would obey; or, rather, because she would obey, she therein ruling."

This halcyon repose is rudely broken by the summons which Argalus feels imperious upon his honor. He resists, with the tenderness of a true hero, the tears and entreaties of his wife, and sallies forth to the fight. After a long and ardent combat, in which miracles of valor are achieved on both sides, he falls mortally wounded, and Parthenia, who has made her way to the scene of action, receives his parting breath. A few days after, Amphialus is challenged by a newly-arrived knight, called the Knight of the Tomb, who is arrayed in black armor, painted in resemblance of an open grave; the greaves upon his legs painted with crawling worms, and his steed hung with cypress branches. Rushing furiously into the *melèe*, the unknown champion soon meets the death he courts; and as his helmet is unloosed, the long golden locks and fair features betray the loving wife, who has thus thrown away the life no longer to be endured.* The whole story teems with irresistible pathos, and is told in a language that is unexceptionable to even modern taste. Indeed, the book abounds with so many passages of unaffected beauty, that we are insensibly led along through its obsolete orthography, until we are fairly lost amid the peaceful groves of Arcadia, listening to the oaten pipes of its shepherds, or hurrying with its heroes from gentle vows beneath a star-lit sky, to the field where their injuries are redressed, and their valor vindicates the right.† We might multiply quotations of equal

* "Where is the antique glory now become,
That whylome wont in wemen to appeare?
Where be the brave atchievements doen by some?
Where be the batteilles, where the shield and speare,
And all the conquests which them high did reare,
That matter made for famous poets verse?"

† "The waies, through which my weary steps I guyde
In this delightful land of Faëry,
Are so exceeding spacious and wyde,
And sprinckled with such sweet variety
Of all that pleasant is to eare or eye,
That I, nigh ravisht with rare thoughts delight,
My tedious travell doe forget thereby;
And, when I 'gin to feele decay of might,
It strength to me supplies, and chears my dulled spright"

SPENSER'S *Faërie Queene.*

interest through a large volume; but as our object is merely to present a specimen of the work that engaged some of the idle hours of Philip Sidney, we must turn away with this little garland of flowers, regretfully leaving a prairie-full behind. Hastening therefore to the conclusion of the story, we will simply add, that during the prolonged siege the damsels are treated with great barbarity by Cecropia, and each is by a stratagem made to believe that her sister is beheaded before her eyes. Amphialus discovers at length the cruelty of his mother, and in his indignation pursues her with a drawn sword to the roof of the castle. Supposing that he intends to strike her, she throws herself from the parapet, and is, of course, instantly killed; and Amphialus, horror-struck that he has caused his mother's death, falls upon his sabre and dies.

The princesses are restored to their home, and, soon after, just as they are preparing to elope with the young princes who have performed prodigious feats in their behalf, Basilius is accidentally poisoned in such a manner that suspicion falls upon them. They are arrested, and about to be executed, when the King of Byzantium, the father of Pyrocles, appears with a large army, vindicates the princesses, and restores order to Arcadia; the king and queen make mutual confession of their folly, and the lovers are united, and, like all other married people, "live very happily all the rest of their lives."

We cannot close the volume without culling at random a few more of the thoughts that enrich its pages, and indicate the fertility of the mind from which they emanated.

"Give tribute, but not oblation, to human wisdom."

"Longer I would not wish to draw breath, than I may keep myself unspotted of any heinous crime."

"In the clear mind of virtue, treason can find no hiding-place."

"The only disadvantage of an honest heart is credulity."

"The hero's soul may be separated from his body, but never alienated from the remembrance of virtue."

"Doing good is the only certainly happy action of a man's life."

"The journey of high honor lies not in smooth ways."

"Who shoots at the mid-day sun, though he is sure he shall never hit the mark, yet as sure he is, that he shall shoot higher than he who aims but at a bush."

"Remember that in all miseries, lamenting becomes fools, and action, the wise."

"The great, in affliction, bear a countenance more princely than they were wont; for it is the temper of highest hearts, like the palm-tree, to strive most upward when it is most burthened."

"The perfect hero passeth through the multitude as a man that neither disdains a people, nor yet is any thing tickled with their flattery."

"In a brave bosom, honor cannot be rocked asleep by affection."

"Contention for trifles can get but a trifling victory."

"Prefer truth, before the maintaining of an opinion."

"A man of true honor thinks himself greater in being subject to his word given, than in being lord of a principality."

"Joyful is woe for a noble cause, and welcome all its miseries."

"There is nothing evil but what is within us; the rest is either natural or accidental."

"While there is hope left, let not the weakness of sorrow make the strength of resolution languish."

"Who frowns at others' feasts, had better bide away."

"Friendship is so rare, as it is to be doubted, whether it be a thing indeed, or but a word."

"Prefer your friend's profit before your own desire."

"A just man hateth the evil, but not the evil-doer."

"One look (in a clear judgment) from a fair and virtuous woman is more acceptable than all the kindnesses so prodigally bestowed by a wanton beauty."

"It is folly to believe that he can faithfully love, who does not love faithfulness."

"Who doth desire that his wife should be chaste, first be he true; for truth doth deserve truth."

"It is no less vain to wish death than it is cowardly to fear it."

"Every thing that is mine, even to my life, is hers I love, *but the secret of my friend is not mine.*"

We will close with a parting address of friendship, leaving a mine of wealth behind.

"If I bare thee love, for mine own sake; and that our friendship grew because I, for my part, might rejoice to enjoy such a friend; I should now so thoroughly feel mine own loss, that I should call the heaven and earth to witness, how cruelly you rob me of my greatest comfort, (robbing me of yourself,) measuring the breach of friendship by mine own passion. But because indeed I love thee for thyself; and in my judgment judge of thy worthiness to be loved, I am content to build my pleasure upon thy comfort; and then will I deem my hap in friendship, great, when I shall see thee, whom I love, happy; let me be only sure that thou lovest me still; the only price of true affection! Go therefore on, with the guide of virtue, and service of fortune.—Let thy love be loved; thy desires, prosperous; thy escape, safe; and thy journey, easy. Let every thing yield its help to thy desert! For my part, absence shall not take thee from mine eyes; nor afflictions bar me from gladding in thy good; nor a possessed heart keep thee from the place it hath for ever allotted thee. My only friend! I joy in thy presence, but I joy more in thy good. That friendship brings forth the fruits of enmity, which prefers its own tenderness before its friend's advantage. Farewell!"

Horace Walpole, with characteristic flippancy, pronounced the Arcadia a "tedious, lamentable pastoral." He either never read it, or had not the discernment to see its merits. In Sidney's own day, and long after, it was the favorite romance of the courtiers and ladies of England; it went through fourteen editions, and was translated into several languages. Shakspeare borrowed many incidents from it; Sir Walter Raleigh made it the companion of his prison hours; eminent writers of the next century repeatedly allude to it with praise, and many of the pretty conceits for which later writers receive credit, may be traced back to its glittering pages. Cowper writes in the Task:

> "Would I had fallen upon those happier days
> That poets celebrate, those golden times
> And those Arcadian scenes, that Maro sings,
> And Sidney, warbler of poetic prose."

The pastoral songs and comic plays interspersed through the book are unworthy of the rest; but they are not linked with the story, and are only a tribute to the still crude taste of the Elizabethan age. The varied emotions of the human heart, the fervor of love and truth of friendship, are portrayed in their purest and highest form; and to the simple earnestness of nature is added the ideal grandeur of imagination. It is not only as a reflection of the mind of Sir Philip Sidney that the Arcadia is valuable, but as a rich field of poetic thought and imagery, for the reward of the careful gleaner. In the public library, plethoric with the lore of nations, this quaint old quarto may rest upon its own peculiar merits; although, it must be admitted, they often seem to be hopelessly buried in sentences which are involved, pedantic, and like the apparel of the times, cumbered with tinsel and embroidery. It was not intended by Sidney for publication, and, in fact, it did not appear in print until after his death. Written merely to beguile his leisure hours at Wilton, and to please the sister whom he tenderly loved, he expresses a fear in the preface to her that, "like the spider's web, it will be thought only fit to be swept away." "You desired me to do it, and your desire to my heart is an absolute commandment. It is not for severer eyes, being but a trifle, and triflingly handed."—"Your dear self can best witness the manner; being done in loose sheets, most of it in your presence."

We conclude this chapter with an interesting extract from the London Athenæum, Jan. 2, 1858,—

"In an old folio copy of the Arcadia, preserved at Wilton, have been found two beautiful and interesting relics,—a lock of Queen Elizabeth's hair, and an original poem, in the hand of Sir Philip Sidney. The hair was given by the fair hands of the Queen to her young hero. The poet repaid the precious gift in the following lines:—

'Her inward worth all outward worth transcends,
Envy her merits with regret commends;

Like sparkling gems her virtues draw the light,
And in her conduct she was always bright.
When she imparts her thoughts her words have force,
And sense and wisdom flow in sweet discourse.'

"The date of this exchange of gifts was 1583, when the Queen was forty, and the Knight, twenty-nine.

"Elizabeth's hair is very fine, soft and silky, with the undulation of water; its color, a fair auburn or golden brown, without a tinge of red, as her detractors assert, but the soft lines are flecked with light, and shine as though powdered with gold dust. In every country under the sun, such hair would be pronounced beautiful."

CHAPTER VIII.

RETURNING to the annals of the life of Philip Sidney, we infer that he remained at Wilton until 1581, when he represented in Parliament his native county of Kent, and is sometimes incidentally mentioned as a member of select committees on important subjects. He was now widely known as a chivalrous and patriotic man, with the will to do and the soul to dare whenever the right required defence or the wrong demanded redress. He had not, it is true, performed any startling acts of heroism; nor had applauding multitudes borne him in the triumphal car, or crowned him with the bays of the victor; but his capacities for action in any glorious arena, were as manifest to those who knew him as is the strength of a giant in his repose. He was urged by two military leaders on the continent to join their enterprises. One was Prince Casimir, who conducted to the aid of Holland an army of German mercenaries, under the pay and patronage of Queen Elizabeth.

Another was Don Antonio, one of the seven claimants to the throne of Portugal, after the death of Henry V. Sidney wisely declined both these invitations. Casimir was an obstinate, reckless adventurer, and his marauding troops only pillaged the country they had engaged to protect. The Portuguese insurgent had no just claim to the crown, and neither the wisdom nor the nerve to sustain its assumption. The long talons of that neighboring bird of prey, Philip II., quietly clutched the kingdom, and the discrowned monarch retired to Paris, and died of grief for its loss.

A painful event to Sidney, about this time, was the death of his friend Languet. Two years before, the latter visited England for the sole purpose of seeing one whom he loved with parental fondness and watched with parental care. Distinguished attention was offered him by the English, whom he pronounced the happiest nation in Christendom. He was greatly revered by his own countrymen; and Dr. Zouch says that "the history of his life would be the history of Europe for near a century, as none of his rank in society had a more powerful influence in the direction of public affairs." * All the eminent authors of the day gave to his learning and his

* Zouch's Life of Sir Philip Sidney.

moral merit their concurrent praise; and Mornay Du Plessis wrote of him, "He was in reality what many wish to appear to be; he lived as the best of men should die."

This truly illustrious man was buried at Antwerp with great ceremony, William of Orange acting as chief mourner.

But, hand in hand, Tragedy and Comedy walk the world together. As the one flings open the door of the sepulchre, the other rings in his ear the silver bells of mirth. From the grave of Languet, to which his mournful fancy wandered, Sidney was summoned to take part in one of those displays of knight-errantry which constituted so marked a feature of Elizabeth's reign, and were intended chiefly as censers for the incense that was her vital element. Not content that every man should kneel as he entered her presence—Lord Burleigh only being exempted in his later years on account of the gout—and not satiated with the servile homage constantly breathed to her in private, she sometimes expected a shower of public flatteries.

The pause in her matrimonial negotiations, after the letter of Philip Sidney, was farther extended by the civil discords of France, which, with his own intrigues for the government of the Netherlands, so occupied the Duke of Anjou as to leave him little time for dalliance in unrewarded lovemaking. But Simiers, the subtle pleader, was left in England to watch the progress of affairs, and to carry significant messages back and forth; and so cleverly did he brush away from his master's portrait the gathering dust of time, that its attractions really seemed to brighten with the lapse of years. In October, 1581, Anjou, resolving upon a final master-stroke, sent over a splendid legation to bring matters to a close. The "crowned nymph" as poor Stubbs called her, chose to receive the French peers in a sort of fairy palace which she had built for the occasion at Whitehall, and there she entertained them with banquets and pageants, while her ministers were preparing the marriage articles. This spacious structure was built of timber and canvas, and lighted by nearly three hundred windows, and on each side were ten galleries for spectators. The walls were spangled with gold, and hung with festoons of fruits, flowers, and garlands of ivy and bay leaves. The lofty dome was painted blue, to imitate the sky, where the commingling of stars, sunbeams, and clouds, with the royal arms must have suggested the idea of a general eruption in the firmament.

Beside the tilts and tourneys, and other entertainments, an allegorical device, called a triumph, was enacted by several of the young courtiers, among whom was Philip Sidney, whose presence seemed necessary to give the finishing touch to every festal rite. Let us fancy the long galleries filled with lovely women and gallant cavaliers in their grandest ruffs and most elaborate hose and doublets, while bands of music pour sweet harmonies upon the air. At one end of the tilting-ground is a lofty castle or fortress, termed the Castle of Perfect Beauty, and in it, visible to all the crowd sits the Queen, still fair and handsome, and smiling blandly on the gay illusion. Six trumpeters enter the enchanted circle, and announce the first of four knights who propose to attack the fortress, and obtain possession of its prize. The Earl of Arundel, in gilt armor and on a richly caparisoned steed, leads the van, attended by four pages and twenty squires, all of whom are draped in yellow doublets, crimson velvet hose trimmed with gold lace, and crimson velvet hats with gold bands and yellow feathers. Thirty yeomen follow, dressed in the same colors, of less costly material.

Then rides in Lord Windsor, also in gilt armor; his four pages and twenty-four gentlemen in short cloaks of scarlet, and doublets and hose of tawny orange, black velvet hats with silver bands and white feathers, silvered rapiers and scabbards of black velvet; and his trumpeters and threescore yeoman in similar array.

* "Then proceeded Maister Philip Sidneie, in verie sumptuous manner, with armor, part blew, and the rest gilt and engraven, with foure spare horsses, having caparisons and furniture verie rich and costlie, as some of cloth of gold imbrodered with pearle, and some imbrodered with gold and silver feathers, verie richlie and cunninglie wrought; he had foure pages that rode on his four spare horsses, who had cassocke coats and venetian hose, all of cloth of silver, laied with gold lace, and hats of the same with gold bands and white feathers, and each one a paire of white buskins. Then had he thirtie gentlemen and yeomen, and foure trumpetters who were all in cassock coats, and venetian hose of yellow velvet laied with silver lace, yellow velvet caps with silver bands and white feathers, and everie one a paire of white buskins; and they had upon their coats a scrowle or band of silver, which came scarf-wise over the shoulder, and so down under the arme, with this posie or sentence written upon it, both before and behind, '*Sic nos non nobis.*' " †

* Hollinshed's Chronicles.

† "Thus are we, but not for ourselves"—probably intending to express the idea that he jested to amuse others, rather than himself.

Sir Fulke Greville brings up the rear in equal splendor, his attendants being apparalled in orange and gold.

After various brilliant evolutions, and a number of long harangues, in which the Castle of Beauty is summoned to surrender, and of course refuses, a grand assault is made upon it by means of scaling-ladders, cannons loaded with sweet powders and perfumes, flowers, love-letters, and similar deadly weapons. Several other knights come to aid the besiegers, two of them representing Adam and Eve in armor, decorated with painted apples and figleaves, and helmets covered with long hair. Another, with dishevelled locks and woful gestures, personates Despair. But the fortress proves invulnerable, and at length each assailant presents an olive-branch to the Queen, in token of submission. Her Majesty graciously thanks the combatants, and is pleased with the gay masquerade that testifies to the French ambassadors the loyalty and admiration of her subjects.

The arrival of the Duke multiplied these nuptial festivities, in which, as Motley says, "nothing was omitted but the nuptials." For several months, the Queen played the drama of caprice which had long kept her subjects and her suitor in perpetual agitation, until the latter hastily took his departure, irritated beyond endurance by her pitiful vacillation, and tired of a ten years' chase after the *ignis fatuus* of a crown. The States of Belgium had given him a limited sovereignty, with the title of Duke of Brabant, in the hope of securing for themselves religious toleration and defence against the tyranny of Spain; his prospective alliance with Elizabeth, seeming to promise the united protection of England and France. He was accompanied, on his return thither, by a brilliant *cortége* of English gentlemen of high degree, sent by the Queen in token of her good will.

The Lords Hunsdon, Howard, and Leicester, Philip Sidney, and a hundred or two besides, landed at Flushing with the Duke and his own splendid retinue. William of Orange, the ever-faithful sentinel, was there to greet him with a large deputation; and amid music, artillery, and acclamations, they were escorted to an elegant banquet, which was furnished with the same astonishing prodigality of sugar utensils and ornaments as were those given in Venice to Henry III. of France. After a week of gala days and nights, they were all conveyed in fifty-four vessels to Antwerp, and made an imposing *entrée* into that opulent capital. The military companies in their bright uniforms, the Hanseatic merchants in their old German costume, the city functionaries in black velvet and gold chains, and the cavalcade of illustrious men from three neighboring countries, marched in stately procession through triumphal arches, flashing torches, and bands of martial music; and for many days orations were delivered, compliments exchanged, and allegories acted, until everybody must have been exhausted, and the English lords very glad to set sail homeward.

Through all these glittering ceremonials, Sidney found time for extensive reading, and constant association with men of letters, of whom he was ever the liberal patron. He accumulated a large and choice library, employing agents to purchase for him at the annual fairs in Leipsic, Frankfort, and other towns. We read continually of books that were dedicated to him by the most distinguished authors of England, Germany, and France. Scipio Gentilis, a professor of law in Oxford, and celebrated as a Latin versifier, addressed him in this eulogistic strain:—

"Others admire in you, Philip Sidney, the splendor of your birth—your genius in your childhood, capable of all philosophy—your honorable embassy undertaken in your youth, and the experience obtained from visiting the cities and viewing the manners of so many countries—

the exhibition of your personal valor and prowess in the public spectacles and equestrian exercises, in your manhood;—let others admire all these qualities. I not only admire, but I love and venerate you, because you regard poetry so much as to excel in it; nor will I omit any opportunity of acknowledging my obligations to you, as far as it is in my power."

Banco, a learned theologian, inscribes to Sidney his biography of the distinguished philosopher Ramus, who, as heretofore stated, was one of the victims of the massacre at Paris. "Without flattery," he says, "I pronounce you to be a perfect image and resemblance of nobility. For, not to mention your descent from the family of the Earls of Warwick, eminently illustrious throughout all England, your virtue, outshining the splendor of an high lineage, seems to me a theme of just encomium. I remember well, when I first saw you, when I first contemplated with wonder your uncommon endowments of mind and body; I remember well, I say, the words of Gregory, who declared the Angli, or English, that were at Rome, to be really angels." If this sounds like fulsome panegyric, we must remember that it was a hearty and honest sentiment, uttered in an age of such comparative simplicity, that language was then used to express thought, and not to conceal it.

A work on military tactics was dedicated to him, because, as the author says, he "found none more forward to further and favor martial knowledge; being of himself most ready and adventurous in all exercises of war and chivalry."

Richard Hakluyt, the renowned cosmographer, inscribed his first collection of voyages to this "most generous promoter of all ingenious and useful knowledge." Lipsius, the scholar and critic, in a similar instance, addressed him as "the bright star of Britain, on whom light is copiously diffused by Virtue, by the Muses, by the Graces, and by Fortune."

Sidney never saw the noontide glory of the Elizabethan day of literature. It was now but in the purple dawn, to which his own taste and talent lent many rays of brightness. He was already known as a poet, and very soon he wrote an Essay, called the "Defence of Poesy," which is believed to be the first critical work of merit in the English language. The names of Shakspeare, Ben Johnson, Raleigh, Greene, Drayton, Davies, Chapman, and others, were yet unknown; and, with the exception of Sidney and Spenser, there were no poetical celebrities whose effusions have any interest for modern readers.

The author of the "Faërie Queen" was born to that frequent inheritance of genius—poverty;

but the friendship which he formed at Oxford with Sidney and Raleigh, and the patronage of the Earl of Leicester, had secured his present exemption from those sordid cares that so vex the poet's soul. The first was a most kind and generous friend; he invited him to Penshurst, where they spent several weeks together, and induced him to transfer his attention from pastoral to heroic verse. Mankind are probably indebted to this piece of advice for that grand and vivid epic which has given delight to them, and renown to its creator. The early portions of the "Faërie Queen" were submitted to the criticism of Sir Philip, and there is a story, (not, however, very reliable,) that when he heard the description of Despair, in the ninth canto of the first book, he was so transported with admiration, as to direct his steward to present the author with fifty pounds; when the second stanza was read, he ordered the sum to be doubled; at the third, he called for two hundred pounds, and commanded its immediate payment lest he should be induced to give away all he possessed.

Gabriel Harvey was another learned friend of Sidney, but rather pretentious and pedantic, and only remembered for his attempts to introduce the Latin hexameter into English verse. All his contemporaries were somewhat infected with his example. Sidney followed it, in some of the eclogues of the Arcadia, and even Spenser himself, notwithstanding his admission that the English hexameter has much the effect of "a lame gosling that draweth one leg after her, or of a lame dog that holdeth one leg up."

Sir Fulke Greville, afterward Lord Brooke, was the relative and the most intimate friend of Sidney; they were of the same age, and both allied

"In brave pursuit of chivalrous emprise."

A terrace near the seat of the former in Warwickshire, is still pointed out as the spot where they walked together on summer mornings, and held the genial converse of kindred souls. The poems of Greville, though quite celebrated in their day, are now known only to the curious searchers into literature, their harsh and pedantic style being a cumbrous vehicle for lofty sentiment and ingenious imagery. They consist of two tragedies, and a hundred love sonnets, in one of which he addresses his mistress as "Fair Dog!" He wrote a memoir of his early friend, and, in an inscription which he composed for his own monument, he expressed his love and admiration in the significant climax,

FULKE GREVILLE, SERVANT TO QUEEN ELIZABETH, COUNSELLOR TO KING JAMES, AND FRIEND TO SIR PHILIP SIDNEY."

Even the most unpretending sketch of Sir Philip Sidney would be incomplete without some notice of his "Defence of Poesy," (or as it was termed by him, "Apologie for Poesie,") a work which is justly celebrated as the most finished prose production of that era, and as the basis of numberless dissertations that have since appeared on the same subject. If it seem remarkable that the "divine art" should require defence, it must be remembered that no master hand had touched the lyre in England, since the days of Chaucer and Gower, who lived when Petrarch and Dante woke Italy with its echoes. The few subsequent poets, though not destitute of merit, had done nothing to sustain its dignity or elevate its tone. In an age that with the chivalric spirit of the past, singularly blended great intellectual activity, laborious research, and a freedom of speech which has been almost refined away in our more fastidious civilization, it is not surprising that satirists were numerous, keen, and critical. The Puritans, too, with all the zeal of a new-born sect, anathematized poetry in merciless measure. A creature born in sin and meriting perdition, they argued, should devote his hours to penance and prayer, not to syren melodies and carnal songs of pleasure. The pilgrim through a vale of tears, had no right to prate of the allurements of beauty, or dream amid the chimeras of an unholy brain. In the judgment of these stern old reformers, as sorcery bewitched the people, so poetry bewitched language. Scorning, as they did, both the authority and the vices of aristocracy, they equally scorned its refinements and its culture. Thus the glowing words of passion and of love, stirred into rhyme and rhythm by the poet's wand, seemed to them allied to the sensual more than to the intellectual, and to be figments of heathen philosophy, rather than emanations of Christian intelligence.

It was to combat both the carping critics and the sturdy reformers, that this young champion sallied forth, armed with the simple but effective weapons of reason and of truth. Of his success we leave our readers to judge.

He begins by the announcement that having "slipped into the title of a poet," he desires to say something in defence of "that art which, from almost the highest estimation of learning, is fallen to be the laughing-stock of children." He alludes to its antiquity, and argues that in all countries it "opens the portals to all other knowledge." Musaeus, Homer, and Hesiod were the fathers of Grecian learning; the fables of Amphion and Orpheus were tributes to musical verse; Dante, Petrarch, and Boccaccio made Italy the "treasure-house of science;" Chaucer and Gower were the morning stars of England's day of song. The philosophers of Greece garlanded their philosophy with the flowers of poesy, and Herodotus added the charm of poetic fiction to win attention to his facts. In Wales, poetry had outdone all art and science; "in Ireland, where learning goes very bare, yet are their poets held in devout reverence. Even among the most barbarous and simple Indians, where no writing is, yet have they their poets, who sing of their ancestors' deeds, and praises of their gods." He speaks of the high esteem in which the poet was held in Rome, being called Vates, a diviner or prophet; and alludes to the "heavenly poesie" of the Hebrew Psalmist. He proceeds to contrast the art with other arts and sciences:—

"There is no art delivered unto mankind, that hath not the works of Nature for its principal object, without which they could not consist, and on which they so depend, as they become Actors and Players, as it were, of what Nature will have set forth. So doth the Astronomer look upon the stars, and that he hath set down what order Nature hath taken therein. So doth the Arithmetician and Geometrician in their divers sorts of quantities. So doth the Musician, in tunes, tell you which by Nature agree, which not. The natural Philosopher thereon hath his name, and the moral Philosopher standeth upon the natural virtues, vices, or passions of man; and follow nature, saith he, therein, and thou shalt not err. The Lawyer saith what men have determined. The Historian, what men have done. The Grammarian speaketh only of the rules of speech; and the Rhetorician and Logician, considering what in nature will soonest prove and persuade, thereon give artificial rules, which still are compassed within the circle of a question, according to the proposed matter. The Physician weigheth the nature of man's body, and the nature of things helpful or hurtful unto it. And the Metaphysicke, though it be in the second and abstract motions, and therefore be accounted supernatural, yet doth he indeed build upon the depth of Nature."

He follows these accurate distinctions of the material world with an enthusiastic picture of the ideal realm whose golden gates the poet only may unbar.

"Only the Poet, disdaining to be tied to any

such subjection, lifted up with the vigor of his own invention, doth grow in effect into another nature; in making things either better than nature bringeth forth, or quite a new form, of such as never were nature; as the Heroes, Demi-gods, Cyclops, Chimeras, Furies, and the like; so as he goeth hand in hand with nature, not inclosed within the narrow warrant of her gifts, but freely ranging within the zodiac of his own wit. Nature never set forth the earth in so rich tapestry, as divers Poets have done, neither with so pleasant rivers, fruitful trees, sweet-smelling flowers, nor whatsoever else may make the too much loved earth more lovely; her world is brazen, the Poets only deliver a golden."

He then enumerates with great clearness the various kinds of poets, the religious, the philosophical, and those that "justly may be called *Vates*, who range only into the divine consideration, and what may be, and should be." "It is not rhyming and versing," he adds, "that make a Poet, (no more than a long gown maketh an advocate, who, though he pleaded in armor should be an advocate and no soldier,) but is that joining notable images of virtues, vices, or what else, with that delightful teaching, which must be the right describing note to know a Poet by."

——"The end of all earthly learning being virtuous action, those skills that most serve to bring forth that, have a most just title to be princes over the rest; wherein we easily can show, the Poet is worthy to have it before any other competitors. Among whom principally to challenge, step forth the Moral Philosophers; whom methinks I see coming towards me with a sullen gravity, (as they could not abide vice by daylight,) rudely clothed, for to witness outwardly their contempt of outward things, with books in their hands against glory, whereto they set their name; sophistically speaking against subtlety, and angry with any man in whom they see the foul fault of anger. These men, casting largess as they go of definitions, divisions, and distinctions, with a scornful interrogative do soberly ask, whether it be possible to find any path so ready to lead a man to virtue as that which teacheth what virtue is."——"The Historian scarcely gives leisure to the Moralist to say so much, but that he, loaden with old mouse-eaten records, authorizing himself for the most part upon other histories, whose greatest authorities are built upon the notable foundation of *Hear-say*, having much ado to accord differing writers, and to pick truth out of partiality; better acquainted with a thousand years ago than with the present age, and yet better knowing how this world goes, than how his own wit runs; curious for antiquities, and inquisitive of novelties, a wonder to young folks, and a tyrant in table-talk;—denieth, in a great chafe, that any man for teaching of virtue is comparable with him." ——"The Philosopher, setting down with thorny arguments the bare rule, is so hard of utterance, and so misty to be conceived, that one who hath no other guide but him, shall wade in him till he be old, before he shall find sufficient cause to be honest. For his knowledge standeth so upon the abstract and general, that happy is that man who may understand him, and more happy that can apply what he doth understand. On the other side, the Historian, wanting the precept, is so tied, not to what should be, but to what is, to the particular truth of things, and not to the general reason of things, that his example draweth no necessary consequence, and therefore a less fruitful doctrine. Now doth the peerless Poet perform both; for whatsoever the Philosopher saith should be done, he gives a perfect picture of it by some one, by whom he presupposeth it was done, so as he couples the general notion with the particular example."

"Tully taketh much pains, and many times

not without poetical helps, to make us know the force love of our country hath in us. Let us but hear old Anchises speaking in the midst of Troy's flames, or see Ulysses in the fulness of all Calypso's delights, bewail his absence from barren and beggarly Ithaca. Anger, the Stoics said, was a short madness; let but Sophocles bring you Ajax on a stage, killing or whipping sheep and oxen, thinking them the army of Greeks, with their chieftains Agamemnon and Menelaus; and tell me if you have not a more familiar insight into anger, than finding in the schoolmen its genus and difference."

"Now therein of all sciences is our Poet the Monarch. For he doth not only shew the way, but giveth so sweet a prospect, as will entice any man to enter into it; Nay, he doth as if your journey should lie through a fair vineyard, at the very first give you a cluster of grapes, that full of that taste, you may long to pass further. He beginneth not with obscure definitions, which must blur the margin with interpretations, and load the memory with doubtfulness; but he cometh to you with words set in delightful proportion, either accompanied with, or prepared for, the well-enchanting skill of music, and with a tale forsooth he cometh unto you, with a tale which holdeth children from play, and old men from the chimney corner; * and pretending no more, doth intend the winning of the mind from wickedness to virtue; even as the child is often brought to take most wholesome things by hiding them in such other as have a pleasant taste."

"By these examples and reasons, I think it may be manifest, that the Poet, with that same hand of delight, doth draw the mind more effectually than any other Art doth. And so a conclusion not unfitly ensues; that as virtue is the most excellent resting-place for all worldly learning to make its end of, so Poetry being the most familiar to teach it, and most princely to move towards it, in the most excellent work, is the most excellent workman."

Here he presents at length the relative value and beauty of the various forms of poetry;—the pastoral, the elegiac, the comic, the tragic, the lyric,—and enthusiastically dilates upon the union of metre with music:—

"I never heard the old song of Percie and Douglas, that I found not my heart moved more than with a trumpet; and yet it is sung by some blind crowder, with no rougher voice, than rude

* This is supposed to be the origin of Shakspeare's—

"That elder ears played truant at his tale,
And younger hearings were quite ravished,—
So sweet and voluble was his discourse," &c.

style; which being so evil apparelled in the dust and cobweb of that uncivil age, what would it work, trimmed in the gorgeous eloquence of Pindar? In Hungary, I have seen in the manner of all feasts, and other such like meetings, to have songs of their ancestors' valor, which that soldier-like nation think one of the chiefest kindlers of courage. The incomparable Lacedæmonians did not only carry that kind of Music ever with them to the field; but even at home, as such songs were made, so were they all content to be singers of them; when the lusty men were to tell what they did, the old men, what they have done, the young men, what they would do."

"Since then," he sums up the argument, "Poetry is of all human learning the most ancient, and of most fatherly antiquity;—since it is so universal that no learned nation doth despise it, nor barbarous nation is without it; since both Roman and Greek gave such divine names unto it, the one of prophesying, the other of making; and that indeed the name of making is fit for him, considering that where all other Arts retain themselves within their subject, and receive, as it were, their being from it, the Poet only bringeth his own stuff, and doth not learn a Conceit out of a matter, but maketh matter for a Conceit. Since neither his description nor end containeth any evil, the thing described cannot be evil, since his effects be so good as to teach goodness, and delight the learners of it; since therefore, (namely, in moral doctrine, the chief of all knowledges,) he doth not only far surpass the Historian, but for instructing is wellnigh comparable to the Philosopher; since the holy Scripture hath whole parts in it poetical, and that even our Saviour Christ vouchsafed to use the flowers of it; since all his kindnesses are not only in their united forms, but in their several directions fully commendable, I think, (and think I think rightly,) the Laurel Crown appointed for triumphant Captains, doth worthily, of all other learnings, honor the Poet's triumph."

He proceeds to canvass the objections against poetry; just the objections of the stoics of old and the utilitarians of to-day; of men who would measure the soul by the limited compass of reason, and reduce life to a practical demonstration; who would stifle the yearnings of love, strangle the generous impulse, and dissipate the heaven-born phantoms of beauty and of taste. We will not follow Sir Philip Sidney's argument, because, as we have before stated, it has had so many admirers, and so many plagiarists, that under other guises its face is universally familiar. It is enough to say that its accuracy of reasoning and sustained dignity of thought are richly adorned with the flowers of fancy, and with classical illustration, while, in the enthusiasm which pervades the whole "Defence," we see that he wrote in obedience to what he tells us was the mandate of his Muse, "Look in thy heart, and write."

He especially regrets that poetry has fallen from its high esteem in England; and gives, as the cause, that "base men with servile wits undertake it, who think it enough if they be rewarded of the printer; and so, as Epaminondas is said with the honor of his virtue to have made an office by his exercising it, which before was contemptible, to become highly respected; so these men no more but setting their names to it, by their own disgracefulness, disgrace the most graceful Poesie."—"As the fertilest ground must be manured," he says again, "so must the highest plying wit have a Dædalus to guide him."

He winds up this "hymn of intellectual beauty," as it has been well pronounced, by the following eloquent peroration:—

"So that since the ever praiseworthy Poesie is full of virtue, breeding delightfulness, and void of no gift that ought to be in the noble name of learning, since the blames laid against it are either false or feeble, since the cause why it is not esteemed in England is the fault of Poet apes, not Poets; since lastly our tongue is most fit to honor Poesie, and to be honored by Poesie, I conjure you all that have had the ill luck to read this ink-wasting toy of mine, even in the name of the nine Muses, no more to scorn the sacred mysteries of Poesie; no more to laugh at the name of Poets, as though they were next inheritor to fools; no more to jest at the reverent title of a rhymer, but to believe with Aristotle that they were the ancient treasurers of the Grecian divinity; to believe with Bembus that they were first bringers in of all civility; to believe with Scaliger that not philosopher's precepts can sooner make you an honest man, than the reading of Virgil; to believe with Clauserus, the translator of Cornutus, that it pleased the heavenly deity by Homer and Hesiod, under the veil of fables to give us all knowledge, Logic, Rhetoric, Philosophy, natural and moral, and *Quid non?* To believe with me that there are many mysteries contained in Poetry, which of purpose were written darkly, lest by profane wits it should be abused; to believe with Landin that they are so beloved of the gods, that whatsoever they write, proceeds out of a divine fury. Lastly, to believe themselves when they tell you they will make you immortal by their verse. Thus doing, your names shall flourish in the printer's shops; thus doing, you shall be of kin to many a poetical preface; thus doing, you shall be most fair, most rich, most wise, most all; you shall dwell upon superlatives; thus doing, though you be *Libertino patre natus*, you shall suddenly grow *Herculea proles, si quid mea carmina possunt.* Thus doing, your soul shall be placed with Dante's Beatrix, or Virgil's Anchises. But if (fie of such a But) you be born so near the dull-making cataract of Nilus, that you cannot hear the planet-like music of Poetry; if you have so earth-creeping a mind, that it cannot lift itself up to look to the skies of Poetry; then, though I will not wish unto you the asses' ears of Midas, nor to be driven by a Poet's verses as Bubonax was to hang himself, nor to be rhymed to death, as is said to be done in Ireland, yet thus much curse I must send you in the behalf of all Poets, that while you live you live in love, and never get favor, for lacking skill of a sonnet; and when you die, your memory die from the earth for want of an epitaph."

"In this luminous criticism and effusion of poetic feeling," remarks D'Israeli, "Sidney has introduced the principal precepts of Aristotle, touched by the fire and sentiment of Longinus;

and for the first time in English literature, has exhibited the beatitude of criticism in a poet-critic."*

In concert with his sister, Sir Philip wrote a Paraphrase of the Psalms of David. The last work that occupied his pen was a translation of an Essay by Du Plessis on the Truth of Christianity. It was incomplete at the time of his death.

In the year 1581, the Earl of Leicester made himself very obnoxious to the Papists by his active measures in the discovery and suppression of several conspiracies projected by them against the Queen. His violent denunciations were responded to by an invective from a Jesuit, named Green, consisting of a circumstantial detail of all the crimes which had ever been laid to his charge, intermingled with political reflections upon the connection between his iniquities and the Popish dissatisfaction with the government. This publication was circulated throughout Europe and read in England with the greatest avidity; the efforts made by the Queen for the suppression of statements so prejudicial to her favorite, only increasing its notoriety.

Sir Philip Sidney, with all the pride of affection and of zeal for the family honour, attempted

* Amenities of Literature, vol. ii.

to refute these charges in a letter, which, though ingenious, was by no means conclusive in his uncle's favor, and was marked rather by warmth than by judgment. He probably failed to satisfy himself, as his work was unpublished until its appearance many years after in the Sidney Papers.*

* Lodge's Illustrious Personages.

CHAPTER IX.

IN presenting to our readers a few selections from the sonnets of Sir Philip Sidney, it is needless to suggest that they must not be judged by the standard of modern cultivation. His talents and his virtues would have shown brightly even in this resplendent century; for such talents are always rare, and such virtues are of all time: but their manifestation must be viewed through the focal distance of three hundred years, and amid the crude taste and quaint accompaniments which we have endeavored to portray. Therefore we bespeak from those who for Sidney's sake have followed us thus far, and who like Bacon are "glad to light" their "torch at any man's candle," a just appreciation of the dainty hyperboles, the feeling and the pathos that sparkle like crystals through the rough metre and obsolete iteration. We have hitherto gathered the scattered fragments of Sir Philip's outer and worldly life. We have aimed to sketch him as a dutiful son, a loving brother, a true friend; as a patriot, a scholar, and an accomplished cavalier. We have shown the dazzling versatility of the genius with which courts were delighted, and fair women charmed; which statesmen applauded, and critics could not condemn.

> "Beloved over all,
> In whom it seems that gentleness of spright
> And manners mild were planted natural;
> To which he, adding comely guise withal,
> And gracious speech, did steal men's hearts away." *

But we have not unveiled the golden affections that were enshrined far beneath the surface, sacred from the storms, unmoved by the tides of material elements. Every life has its hidden romance, every soul worships, ofttimes unconsciously, its shadowy ideal of human loveliness. The romance of Sidney's heart is revealed in the sonnets, which, under the *nom de plume* of "Astrophel," he addressed to "Stella." Her real name was Penelope Devereux; she was the daughter of Walter, Earl of Devereux, and the sister of that Earl of Essex, to whom both the love and the anger of the Queen seemed equally fatal.

Sidney had known this lady from her childhood, and soon after his return from his travels, a union was proposed between them, and some of their

* Faërie Queen.

friends were very anxious for its accomplishment. Sir Edward Waterhouse wrote to Sir Henry Sidney: "All the lords that wish well to the children of the Earl of Essex, and I suppose all the best sorte of the English lords besides, doe expect what will become of the treaty between Mr. Phillip and my Lady Penelope. Truly, I must say, as I have said to my Lord of Leicester and Mr. Phillip, the breaking off from this match, if the default be on your parts, will turn to more dishonor than can be repaired with any other marriage in England." *

The Egeria of his youth, whom he made

> "Famous by his pen,
> And glorious by his sword,"

was a leading star in the world of rank and fashion, and is described as a woman of almost faultless beauty, of graceful, yet commanding figure, light brown hair, a clear, vivid complexion, and lustrous, dark eyes. He alludes to those beguiling eyes in describing a tilting match, in which he attributes his success to their encouraging glances:

> "Having this day my horse, my hand, my lance
> Guided so well, that I obtained the prize,
> Both by the judgment of the English eyes,
> And of some sent from that sweet enemy, France;

* Collin's Sidney Papers.

Horsemen my skill in horsemanship advance;
Town-folks, my strength; a daintier Judge applies
His praise to sleight, which from good use doth use;
Some lucky wits impute it but a chance;

Others, because of both sides I doe take
My blood from them who did excel in this,
Think nature me a man of arms did make.

How far they shot awry! the true cause is
STELLA looked on, and from her heavenly face
Sent forth the beams, which made so fair my race."

He often alludes to the expression of modesty and delicate reserve, which lent to those sweet eyes an added fascination:—

"O eyes which doe the spheares of beauty move,
Whose beames be joyes, whose joyes all vertues be;
Who, while they make Love conquer, conquer Love,
The schools where Venus might learn chastity."

And again:—

"Soules joy, bend not those morning starres from me,
Where vertue is made strong by beautie's might,
Where love is chastnesse, paine dothe learne delight,
And humbleness growes one with Majestie.

Whatever may ensue, O let mee be
Copartner of the riches of that sight;
Let not mine eyes be driven from that light;
O looke! O shine! O let me die and see!"

The incense of his homage is offered less to her surpassing loveliness of person, than to the moral purity which it enshrined.

"Who will in fairest book of nature know
How vertue may best lodged in beautie be,
Let him but learne of Love to read in thee,
STELLA, those faire lines, which true goodness show.

There shall we find all vices overthrow,
Not by rude force, but sweetest soveraigntie
Of reason, from whose light those night-birds flye;
That inward sunne in thine eyes shineth so.

And not content to be Perfection's heire
Thyselfe, dost strive all mindes that way to move,
Who marke in thee what is in thee most faire.
So while thy beauty drawes the heart to love,
As fast thy vertue bends that love to good."

Every one remembers Charles Lamb's beautiful Essay upon Sidney's sonnets, in which he says: "We must be lovers,—or at least the cooling touch of time, the *circum præcordia frigus*, must not have so damped our faculties as to take away our recollection that we were once so,—before we can duly appreciate the glorious vanities and graceful hyperboles of the passion." Here again our poet's numbers breathe the romance of true devotion, tinctured, perhaps, with the melancholy always attendant on acute feeling:—

"STELLA, think not that I by verse seek fame,
Who seek, who hope, who love, who live but thee;
Thine eyes my pride, thy lips mine history!
If thou praise not, all other praise is shame

Nor so ambitious am I, as to frame
A nest for my young praise in Lawrell-tree;
In truth I sweare, I wish not there should be
Grav'd in mine epitaph a Poet's name.

Ne if I would, I could just title make,
That any laud to me thereof should grow,
Without my plumes from other wings I take.
For nothing from my wit or will doth flow,
Since all my words thy beauty doth indite,
And love doth hold my hand and makes me write."

It is not probable that Stella returned in equal measure this single-hearted constancy of her lover. She seems at one time to have divided the light and shadow of her countenance between himself and the accomplished Sir Charles Blount, afterward Lord Mountjoy. It must have been while grieving from such an eclipse of her favor that he wrote the following apostrophe, which is certainly a gem of poetic conception and melancholy pathos. The London Retrospective Review, a high authority in criticism, says that if Sidney had written nothing but this, he would still deserve to rank among the poets of his country:—

"With how sad steps, O moone, thou climbst the skies,
How silently, and with how wan a face?
What, may it be that even in heavenly place
That busie archer his sharp arrows tries?

"Sure if that long with Love acquainted eyes
Can judge of Love, thou feel'st a Lover's case,
I read it in thy looks, thy languisht grace,
To me that feele the like, thy state descries.

"Then ev'n of fellowship, O moone, tell me
Is constant Love deem'd there but want of wit?
Are beauties there as proud as here they be?
Doe they above love to be lov'd, and yet
Those lovers scorne whom that *Love* doth possesse?
Doe they call *Vertue* there ungratefulnesse?"

He frequently alludes to the pensive wanderings of his thoughts to their own sweet secret, and complains of the curious crowd that eye him with malicious surmise or unsympathizing sneer:

"Because I oft in dark abstracted guise,
Seem most alone in greatest company;
With dearth of words, or answers quite awry,
To them that would make speech of speech arise;

"They deeme, and of their doome the rumour flies,
That poison foule of bubbling pride doth lye
So in my swelling breast, that onely I
Fawne on my selfe, and others doe despise;

"Yet pride I thinke doth not my soule possesse,
Which lookes too oft in his unflattering glasse,
But one worse fault *Ambition* I confesse,
That makes me oft my best friends overpasse,
Unseene, unheard, while thought to highest place
Bends all his *powers*, even unto *Stella's* grace."

"The curious wits seeing dull pensiveness
Bewray itself in my long settled eyes,
Whence those same fumes of melancholy rise,
With idle paines, and missing ayme, doe ghesse.

"Some that know how my spring I did addresse,
Deeme that my Muse some fruit of knowledge plies;
Others, because the Prince my service tryes,
Thinke that I thinke State errours to redresse.

"But harder judges judge Ambition's rage,
Scourge of itselfe, still climbing slippery place,
Holds my young braine captiv'd in golden cage.

"O fooles, or over-wise, alas, the race
Of all my thoughts hath neither stop nor start,
But onely *Stella's* eyes, and *Stella's* heart."

On one occasion, ne gracefully compliments the delicate beauty of complexion which permitted his fair one to dispense with the usual feminine protections against sunshine and air:

"In highest way of heav'n the Sun did ride,
Progressing then from faire twins' golden place:

Having no scarfe of clouds before his face,
But shining forth of heat in his chiefe pride;

"When some faire Ladies by hard promise ty'd,
On horsebacke met him in his furious race,
Yet each prepar'd with fannes' well shading grace,
From that foe's wounds their tender skins to hide;

"STELLA alone, with face unarmed marcht,
Either to doe like him which open shone,
Or careless of the wealth because her owne;

"Yet were the hid and meaner beauties parcht,
Her daintiest, bare went free; the cause was this,
The Sun which others burn'd, did her but kisse."

Every one must sympathize with the petulant fondness of his address to a friend who had lately left her presence, but whose answers to his anxious inquiries of her welfare were tantalizingly vague and unsatisfactory:—

"Be your words made (good Sir) of Indian ware,
That you allow me them by so small rate?
Or doe you curted Spartans imitate?
Or doe you mean my tender eares to spare,

"That to my questions you so totall are?
When I demand of Phœnix, Stella's state,
You say (forsooth) you left her well of late:
O God, thinke you that satisfies my care?

"I would know whether she sit or walke,
How cloath'd, how waited on, sighed she or smil'd,
Whereof, with whom, how often did she talke?

"With what pastime time's journey she beguil'd?
If her lips daign'd to sweeten my poore name?
Say all, and all well said, *still say the same.*"

May not Shakspeare, who evidently read and admired the Arcadia, have borrowed hence a hint for the queries of his Cleopatra?

——"Oh Charmian,
"Where think'st thou he is now? Stands he or sits he?
Or does he walk? Or is he on his horse?
O happy horse, to bear the weight of Antony!"

At length, the caprice that tempers the loveliness of Stella seems to resolve itself into a return of his own devotion, and he thus pours forth the joyous carol of his renovated hope:—

"O joy, too high for my low stile to show;
O blisse, fit for a nobler state than me!
Envie, put out thine eyes lest thou doe see
What oceans of delight in me doe flow.

"My friend, that oft saw through all maskes my woe,
Come, come, and let me poure my selfe on thee;
Gone is the winter of my miserie,
My Spring appeares, O see what here doth grow.

"For Stella hath with words where faith doth shine,
Of her high heart giv'n me the Monarchy:
I, I, O I may say that she is mine.

"And though she give but thus conditionally
This realme of blisse, while vertue's course I take,
No Kings be crown'd, but they some covenants make."

The following sprightly little song was, perhaps, written under the same inspiration :—

"O faire, O sweet, when I doe looke on thee,
In whom all joyes so well agree,
Heart and soule doe dwell in me;
This you heare is not my tongue,
Which once said what I conceived,
For it was of use bereaved,
With a cruel answer strong.
No, though tongue to roofe be cleaved,
Fearing lest he chastised be,
Heart and soule doe sing in me.

"O faire, O sweet, when I doe looke on thee,
In whom all joyes so well agree;
Just accord all musicke makes;
In thee just accord excelleth,
Where each part in such peace dwelleth,
One of other beautie takes.
Since then truth to all mindes telleth,
That in thee lives harmony,
Heart and soule doe sing in me.

"O faire, O sweete, when I doe looke on thee,
In whom all joyes so well agree;
They that heav'n have knowne, doe say
That whoso that grace obtaineth,
To see what faire sight there raigneth,
Forced are to sing alway;
So then since that heav'n remaineth,
In thy face I plainly see,
Heart and soule doe sing in me."

It is difficult to account for Stella's final acceptance of the title and estates of Lord Rich—a man of uncouth appearance, unpleasant address, and always the object of her avowed aversion. The only plausible solution is that of a mercenary disposition on the part of her guardians, for Lord Rich was affluent, and Sidney was without expectations from his father, and merely the heir in reversion of his uncle Leicester. Only those whose hearts have been scorched and seared with the anguish of blighted hopes, whose wine of life has been turned to gall and bitterness, can sympathize with his sorrow when the object of his devotion was suddenly wrested from his possession. He could not cease to love; but that, after her marriage, his love was transformed into a loyal friendship, we have every reason to believe. His own character is the best guarantee that, as he sometimes said, "in a brave bosom, honor cannot be rocked asleep by affection;" and since not detraction itself could presume in his day, and in the very face of his constant and public homage, to asperse his knightly name, it is meet that we, too, should rightly comprehend the nature of his devotion.

Her own impatience at the trammels thus forced upon her, and the deep tenderness, mingled with delicate reserve, with which she continued to regard him, are feelingly pictured in several of his poems. It is almost needless to say, that they were not intended by him for publication, but were written merely to mitigate the fever, or to solace the sadness, of some solitary hour.

That he learned the lesson for which we are told love was given—the lesson which life in its vanities, its griefs, and even in its gladness, perpetually repeats—

"by mortal yearning to ascend
Toward a higher object—"

we do not need assurance, even from the beautiful effusion with which we close these extracts:

"Leave me, O Love, which reachest but to dust,
And thou, my mind, aspire to higher things;
Grow rich in that which never taketh rust;
Whatever fades, but fading pleasure brings.

Draw in thy beams, and humble all thy might,
To that sweet yoke where lasting freedomes be;
Which breaks the clouds, and opens forth the light,
That doth both shine, and give us sight to see.

O take fast hold, let that light be thy guide,
In this small course which birth drawes out to death;
And thinke how ill becometh him to slide,
Who seeketh heav'n, and comes of heav'nly breath.
Then farewell world, thy uttermost I see,
Eternal Love, maintaine thy life in me."

It is sad to trace the history of the peerless beauty, whose name is imperishable, because linked with that of her poet. We cannot forgive her for her coquetry with Lord Mountjoy, while honored with the love of such a man as Sidney; but her conduct after the death of the latter, was so utterly devoid of principle, as to prove that she could never have been entitled to homage so reverent and confiding. Her subsequent life was a tissue of misery and misfortune. While her brother, of whom she was proudly fond, was a prisoner in the Tower, and there yet seemed hope that the Queen might forgive his offences for the sake of the offender, Lady Rich labored unceasingly for his pardon; besieging her Majesty with tearful appeals and written petitions, until refused further audience. After his execution, she was almost heart-broken, and entirely reckless of public opinion. She married Lord Mountjoy in 1605, after obtaining a divorce from Lord Rich for that purpose, but the scandal that preceded and attended the alliance, was so open and severe, as to produce the most unhappy effects upon both parties. The marriage of a divorced wife during the lifetime of her husband, was considered at that time, in England, an outrageous breach of decorum. Archbishop Laud, who performed the ceremony, ever after observed its anniversary as a day of fasting and prayer. Mountjoy, a high-spirited and distinguished man, was unable to endure the infamy of a blot upon his 'scutcheon, and died a year after; and Stella ended her life, a few months later, in solitude and grief.

In 1583, Sir Philip married the only daughter of Sir Francis Walsingham, upon whose "beauty met with virtue," Ben Jonson glowingly dilates. Although Spenser averred, that Stella was the only woman whom Sidney really loved, it may be inferred from some of his poems, addressed to his wife, that he regarded her with affection and esteem.

It seems, by a letter from Walsingham to Hatton, dated March 19th, 1582, that the Queen, true to her usual antipathy to "domestic bliss," was displeased with Sidney's pending marriage. The secretary says, he "had well hoped that his paynfull and faithfulle service done unto her Majestie, would have secured her good lyking thereof," and he begs Hatton to let her know that "the matche is held for concluded, and how just cause he will have to find himself aggrieved if her Majestie still showe her mislike thereof." *

* Wright's Elizabeth.

CHAPTER X.

WE, of this nineteenth century, when science and enterprise have laid bare the remotest nooks of our terrestrial home, even to the ice-bound secrets of hyperborean zones, can hardly fancy the golden mystery which, in 1585, still enshrouded the Western Continent. There yet lived in England a few venerable men who could talk of the incredulity with which, in their boyhood, people listened to the story of the Genoese adventurer, whose chimerical wanderings had led him to an immense and unexplored land, teeming with wealth, and beautiful as Paradise itself. They well remembered, too, the dark forebodings of the aged, the enthusiastic cheers of the young, that rang in the ears of John and Sebastian Cabot, when Henry VII. granted them leave to sail with their own little fleet in search of distant and unknown lands; and the same "old men eloquent" told of the wonder and applause which greeted the daring mariners, when they returned with the map of the coast from Labrador to Albermarle Sound, and vested in England the primal right to the Continent of North America.

From that time onward, the eager eyes of Europe all turned toward the enchanted West. The fisheries of Newfoundland brought wealth and commerce to the English and the French. The freebooters of Spain wrung from the gentle Mexicans their accumulated treasures. The Dutch merchants planted their colonies among the mangrove trees and the gorgeous birds of Surinam. The flag of the fleur de lys announced French possession of the stately forests of Guiana. The standard of Portugal was raised amid the pines and tamarinds of Brazil. Ponce de Leon sought the fountain of perpetual youth among the mulberry groves of Florida. De Soto and his brave comrades, breaking through the solitudes watered by the Ogeechee and the Altamaha, plucked the purple grapes from the banks of the Alabama, and gazed in silent wonder upon the magnificent Mississippi. The wildest fables regarding the new world gained universal credence. Its rivers were said to sparkle with sands of gold; its inhabitants to deck themselves with inestimable gems, of whose value they knew nothing; the dreams of alchemy were there fulfilled, without the aid of crucible and fire; the Elysian fields were not more redolent of fragrance, or prolific in beauty, in every form of fruit and flower. No nation listened with more credulous delight than did the English. At the time of which we write, Frobisher, that model of patient seamen, had recently returned from the last of his three voyages to Labrador and Greenland, bringing each time, however, no richer reward than one or two specimen savages, and heaps of black earth, supposed to contain the precious metal.* Weather-

* Sidney's interest in these enterprises is indicated in a letter to Languet, dated October 1, 1577: . . . "I wrote you a year ago about a certain Frobisher, who, in rivalry of Magellan has explored that sea he supposes to wash the north part of America. It is a marvellous history. After having made slow progress in the past year, he touched at a certain island for the purpose of recruiting himself and his crew. Here, by chance, a young man, one of the ship's company, picked up a piece of earth which he saw glittering on the ground, and showed it to Frobisher, who being engaged in other matters, and not believing that the precious metals were produced in a region so far to the north, considered it of no value. . . The young man kept the earth by him as a memorial of his labour, (for he had no thought of any thing else,) till his return to London. And there, when one of his friends perceived it shining in an extraordinary manner, he made an assay, and found that it was the purest gold, and without any other intermixture of other metal. Wherefore Frobisher went back to the place, last spring, under orders to

beaten tars held forth to gaping crowds in the little alehouses of Falmouth and of Deptford, upon the hazardous excitements of polar navigation, of hidden rocks, unknown currents, rushing

explore that island; and, should it answer his expectation, to proceed no farther. This he has done, and has now returned, bringing his ships, of which he had only three, and those of small size, full laden; and he is said (for they have not yet unloaded) to have brought two hundred tons of ore. He has given it as his decided opinion, that the island is so productive in metals as to seem very far to surpass the country of Peru. There are also six other islands near to this, which seem very little inferior. It is therefore at this time under debate by what means these, our hitherto successful labors, can be still carried on in safety against the attacks of other nations, among whom the Spaniards and Danes seem especially to be considered: the former, as claiming all the western parts by right from the Pope; the latter, as, being more northerly and nearer, and relying on their possession of Iceland, they are better provided with the means of undertaking this voyage. I wish you would send me your opinion on this subject, and at the same time describe the most convenient method of working those ores."

Languet, in his reply, commends the enterprise of Frobisher, but says that he has noticed in Sidney an eagerness for adventure, and he warningly adds: "Do not let the cursed hunger after gold creep into that spirit of yours, into which nothing has been admitted but the love of goodness and the desire of earning the good-will of all men."

Five months after his first notice of the subject, Sidney wrote again: "Frobisher's gold is now melted and does not waterfalls, and moving mountains of ice. Raleigh's colony, under the gallant Sir Richard Grenville, had just landed on the sunny isles of Roanoke, and sent back glowing descriptions of "the goodliest land under the cope of heaven." Francis Drake had immortalized his name by the circumnavigation of the globe; and though the achievement was tarnished by his extensive piracies among the Spanish possessions in the harbors of the Pacific, the Queen had given him her sanction and encouragement. It may be said in his defence, that Spain was in avowed antagonism to England. A band of troops, and large sums of money, had been sent in 1582 to Ireland, to stir up its inhabitants to further rebellion, in revenge of the Queen's assistance to the Netherlands; and the ships of both countries, traversing the high seas for commerce or adventure, delighted to express their national animosity by individual reprisal.

The youth of England were fired with emula-

turn out so valuable as he at first boasted; however, these islands at 62° are not to be despised; but they keep this as a great secret, lest, as you know, the opportunity be forestalled. Nay, more, they expect to be able to cross the sea at the same latitude; so incorrect is the description of the world as given by cosmographers; but if there should be open sea at such a temperature, you perceive it will be of great importance."

tion of enterprise and of wealth, and filled with longings to behold the Eden of the West. Avarice might there slake its fiercest thirst; Romance realize its wildest dreams; Ambition revel in territorial conquest and colonial freedom. It is not surprising that Philip Sidney, with his poetic fancy, his generous impulse, his craving for heroic action, looked with impatient eye from the disappointments, the intrigues, and the restrictions of a court life, towards the land which mystery and distance gilded with twofold charm. He once wrote despondingly to Languet, in regard to the state of Protestant affairs in the Netherlands: "I seem to see our cause withering away, and am now meditating with myself some Indian project."

When Drake was fitting out his second expedition, in the summer of 1585, Sir Philip, in accordance with one of his favorite mottoes, "*Aut viam inveniam aut faciam*,"—I will either find a way or make one,—engaged to associate himself with it, and to equip, from his own purse, both a naval and a land armament. Sir Fulke Greville, who designed to accompany him, declares that his friend meditated a check upon the dangerous power of Spain, by attacking its West India possessions, and that he also projected the foundation of a new and extensive empire, which, redeeming the forests from their solitude, and blending the strength of civilization with the fertility of nature, should offer to the adventurous a broad arena, and to the oppressed a sanctuary; and, by its wise and liberal administration, reëstablish the golden reign of peace.

He says that the scheme was the result of long and serious thought, and was "the exactest model Europe ever saw; a conquest not to be enterprised but by Sir Philip's reaching spirit, that grasped all circumstances and interests."

Sir Fulke was, as we have previously stated, Sidney's most intimate friend, and probably better acquainted with his purposes than any other. We cannot discern, through the dim light of Sir Philip's scant memorials, all the motives by which he was actuated; but it is impossible to believe that the pure principles which had thus far guided his life, were now sacrificed to cupidity or ambition. This project, however, though carried on with great secrecy, was a failure. The Queen, hearing of his intended departure, recalled "her Philip" by a peremptory message, and gave further orders, that if he declined to obey, the entire fleet must be detained. A vexatious mandate, it must be well imagined, however indicative of her partiality; "yet," says Sir Fulke, "did he sit this processe without noise or anger."

It is difficult to account for the persistent refusals of Elizabeth to grant him advancement, either in a foreign land, or in her own service. Her arbitrary dictum had no other explanation than that of the fiat of Louis XIV.: "*Car tel est notre plaisir.*" But Sidney's fault was impetuosity of temper,—a fault almost inseparable from youth and a fervid nature,—and it may have influenced, in some degree, the policy of the cautious queen.

He certainly possessed her esteem, and was the constant subject of her praise. He was one of her favored band of gentlemen pensioners, ranked by Shakspeare superior to earls, and there is casual mention of the gift from her of a living in Wales; she had recently admitted him to her privy council, and conferred on him the honor of knighthood—an honor the more distinguished because, during her entire reign, only six earls and nine barons were elevated to the peerage, and knights were created with great discrimination. But a request, preferred by him in 1582, for the office of master of the ordinance in connection with his uncle, the Earl of Warwick, was refused. That, however, may have been from some special ill humor on the part of Burleigh, to whom the letter was addressed, toward Leicester; and the Queen was probably influenced by him in her decisiŏn, for Sir Philip says: "I learn that her majesty yields gratious heering unto the suit." He adds that he desires it "much more for the being busied in a thing of some serviceable experience, than for any other commoditie, which is but small, that can arise of it."

An apochryphal story has gained credence with many of the writers of Sir Philip's life, that, in 1585, it was proposed to nominate him to the elective crown of Poland, then left vacant, as they assert, by the death of Stephen Battori. They tell us that his royal mistress forbade the intended honor to her knight, with the declaration that "*her* sheep should not be marked with a stranger's brand," and that Sir Philip loyally replied, he "would rather remain the subject of Queen Elizabeth, than accept the highest preferment in a foreign land." This incident, if true, would doubtless have formed a brilliant episode in Sidney's career, but unfortunately for romance, it can have little or no foundation in historical fact. Fulke Greville, his intimate friend and biographer, does not mention it at all. The standard historians, Thuanus, De Thou, Lelevel, in his Histoire de la Polonie, and most others, agree in the assertion that Battori did not die until December, 1586, which was two months after the death of Sidney. The story rests upon the authority of Naunton, whose "Fragmenta Regalia" is rather a collection of anecdotes and the gossip of the times, than a work of reliable veracity. It seems to us by no means improbable, however, that some of Sir Philip's numerous friends may have suggested the presentation of his name to the Electors of Poland, in view of some future election, and that the story of his positive nomination may have arisen from this shadowy presumption.

While thus, day by day, and year by year, Sidney rose to eminence and fame, the unseen shadows of death were drawing near; the drama which developed the latest phase of his character was in rapid preparation.

The seven United Provinces had lost their pillar of light—William of Orange was no more. After escaping numberless perils from the spy, the traitor, and the assassin, he had at last been shot by an insane fanatic, and was now sepulchred in the land he had served so purely, so zealously, with such untiring self-denial, and such consummate wisdom, that his love appears less human than divine. The Republic was shrouded in gloom; its prospects were more alarming than at any previous time, from the commencement of the war. A more pathetic emphasis was attached to the emblem stamped upon the coin of the unhappy state—a little ship struggling without sails or oars against adverse waves, with the motto, "*Incertum quo fata ferant.*" *

The Duke of Anjou, proving recreant to his promised defence, had been dismissed; and soon after ended, in France, a life made up of follies and of failures. Alexander Farnese, Duke of Parma, had conquered nearly the whole of Flanders and Brabant, and triumphantly established the Spanish troops in Ghent, Brussels, and Antwerp, acquiring a numerous fleet by the reduction of the latter city. With the tactics of despair, its citizens cut away their dykes, inundating the country, and sweeping off his magazines; and vainly endeavored to burn the stupendous fortified bridge which he had built across the wide estuary of the Scheldt, for the purpose of preventing their communication with the sea. The city, beautiful and opulent still, despite repeated ravages, was subjected to the most flagrant rapacities. Plunder, fire, massacre, and the flight of twenty thousand of its principal inhabitants, wrought a destruction so rapid and complete, as finds few parallels in history.

The whole confederacy trembled before the

* Uncertain whither Fate may bear me.

accumulating force of the Duke of Parma. Failing in their application for aid from the King of France, they again applied to Queen Elizabeth, offering her the sovereignty of their realm, and entreating her support. She rejected the offer, from the same cautious anxiety to avoid the imputation of encroachment on the rights of Philip II. that had dictated her refusal of a similar petition, a few years before. But, more than ever aware that the safety and welfare of her own kingdom were closely connected with the independence of her affluent commercial neighbors, she now openly espoused their cause. A treaty was concluded in June, 1585, which secured to them the aid of 6,000 troops, paid by herself during the continuance of the war, and the promise of naval assistance, if it should be required. In pledge of subsequent payment, she was to receive the towns of Brille and Flushing, and the Fort of Rammekins. She invested Sir Thomas Cecil, the eldest son of Lord Burleigh, with the command of the strongly fortified island-town of Brille ; and feeling, no doubt, that she must henceforth give a wider scope to the aspiring spirit of Sir Philip Sidney, she appointed him Governor of Flushing. This town was considered, from its position at the mouth of the western Scheldt, one of the most important points in the Netherlands. The last instructions of Charles V. to his son, referred to the particular care which he should employ for its security. After the revolt began, its citizens drove out the Spanish garrison, destroyed the new-laid foundations of their citadel, and with the assistance of the Prince of Orange, and his confederates, planted themselves in an attitude of resistance, which they were still able to maintain.

Sir Philip assumed the duties of his office on the 18th of November. He was welcomed by the Dutch with every mark of distinction, and immediately appointed Colonel of all their regiments. He left his wife, Lady Frances Sidney, at home, until he could make arrangements for her reception there; because, as he wrote to his father-in-law, to whom he gave a power of attorney over the disposition and care of his property, he "might take such a course as would not be fitt for anye of the feminin gender."

The command of the English forces was given to the Earl of Leicester, under the title of General of the Queen's Auxiliaries, and to this was added a control over the navy, paramount to that of the Lord Admiral himself.*

* It is a remarkable evidence of the religious sentiment of the times, that, among the instructions which Leicester re-

He was attended by five hundred of the youthful nobility; adventurous spirits, that burned to aid the Belgian revolt against the tyranny of Philip II. and to win distinction in this famous school of martial discipline. Among the number was the step-son of Leicester, and brother of Sidney's Stella, Robert, Earl of Essex; who, though only nineteen, had already appeared at court, and been received by the Queen with a favor that clearly foreshadowed his predestined position in her regard. Even at this early age, he was conspicuous by his imperious, though graceful, demeanor, and by his personal prodigality.

Leicester was perfectly unfit for this service, having neither the courage, the integrity, nor the military science, which it required. As usual, however, his discriminating mistress was either wilfully or unconsciously blind to his defects. Her partiality painted him, as her own face upon canvas has, by her unartistic decree, descended to us—without shadows. But he had practised so long and so well the dazzling arts of presence and address, that the Provinces were at first deceived as completely as was the Queen. Landing at Flushing with his splendid retinue, he was

ceived, was a special order to require his soldiers "to serve God, and demean themselves religiously."

received by Sir Philip with cordial ceremonial, and by the Belgians universally with the festivities and pomp appropriate to a conquering prince, rather than to the subject of an ally. They followed him with acclamations, and marked his way by triumphal arches; appointed a guard to attend him, and conferred on him the offices of Governor-General, and Commander-in-Chief of the Army and Navy. Doubtless they hoped that homage to the favorite would gratify the Queen, and secure her deeper interest in their behalf, and were both chagrined and alarmed when, with characteristic jealousy, she sent over her Vice-Chancellor, Sir Thomas Heneage, to express her high indignation that such unexampled honors should be bestowed upon a subject whom, as she said, she "had raised out of the dust." Explanations and submissions were hastily returned, but as Leicester retained his authority, we may plausibly infer that she was reluctant to wound his vanity or his ambition, by its withdrawal.

It was not long, however, before the Provinces themselves repented of their generosity. The incapacity of the new Governor to conduct their military affairs, and his arbitrary and unjust interference in the civil administration, filled them with consternation. He laid such restrictions upon their trade that many of their merchants removed from the country. He altered the coin, levied taxes without their consent, and had the moneys delivered, not to their own treasurer, but to one of his appointment, who refused to render them his accounts. He collected large sums for the alleged purpose of paying the troops, who, after all, were so ill paid, that it was difficult to prevent a mutiny. He ejected their own distinguished citizens from offices of trust, and supplanted them with his own minions, many of whom were known as artful and treacherous men. In all respects, he treated them more like a conquered people whose sovereignty he purposed to assume, than as a free and allied republic.*

And now we are called to witness the magnanimous conduct of his admirable nephew; the upright and decisive efforts by which Sir Philip labored to remedy the evils of this miserable administration. Having been appointed general of the English cavalry, he took a very active part in the campaign, supplied the soldiers from his private purse, and encouraged them by his promises and presence; constantly mediated between his uncle and the discontented citizens, and effectually conciliated Count Hohenlo, who was at

* Watson's Philip II.

the head of a rival faction. Leicester himself acknowledged, after Sidney's death, that he sustained his own authority in the Low Countries, through his superior merit.*

In a letter to his uncle, dated Feb. 2, 1586, Sir Philip remonstrates with him on the ill usage of the English soldiers. "It grieves me very much the soldiers are so badly dealt with in your first beginning of government, not only in their pay, but in taking booties from them, as by your Excellency's letter I find." In the same letter he requests that forces may be sent to besiege Steenburg. "I will undertake upon my life either to ruin it, or to make the enemy raise his siege from Grave, or, which I most hope, both." At another time he intimates that "his charges, divers ways, and particularly his horsemen, grow greater than he is able to go through with;" but protests that "so far from desiring gain, he is willing to spend all he can make."

A letter, addressed by him to Secretary Walsingham, reveals to us his own zeal in the Protestant cause, and the inadequate provision made for her army by the Queen; presenting, too, in a very interesting view, as says one of his biographers, "the same Sidney, whose pen had lately

* Fulke Greville.

been dedicated to the soft and sweet relaxation of poesy and pastoral romance, now writing from his tent, amidst the din of war, with the stern simplicity and short-breathed impatience of an old soldier." We subjoin a few extracts:—

"Right Honorable,

"I receave dyvers letters from you, full of the discomfort which I see, and am sorry to see, y[t] yow daily meet with at home; and I think, such is y[e] goodwil it pleaseth you to bear me, y[t] my part of y[e] trouble is something y[t] troubles yow; but I beseech yow, let it not. I had before cast my count of danger, want, and disgrace; and, before God, Sir, it is trew in my hart, the love of y[e] caws doth so far overballance them all, y[t], with God's grace, thei shall never make me weery of my resolution. If her Ma[i] wear the fountain, I wold fear, considering what I daily fynd, y[t] we shold wax dry; but she is but a means whom God useth, and I know not whether I am deceaved, but I am faithfully persuaded, y[t] if she shold w[th]draw herself, other springes wold ryse to help this action: for methinkes I see y[e] great work indeed in hand against the abusers of the world, wherein it is no greater fault to have confidence in man's power, then it is too hastily to despair of God's work. I think a wyse and constant man ought never to greeve whyle he doth plaie, as a man may sai, his own part truly, though others be out; but if himself leav his hold becaws other marriners will be ydle, he will hardly forgive himself his own fault. For me, I can not promis of my own cource, no, not of the . . . . . becaws I know there is a eyer power y[t] must uphold me, or else I shall fall; but certainly I trust I shall not by other men's wantes be drawne from myself; therefore, good Sir, to whome for my particular I am more bownd then to all men besydes, be not troubled with my troubles, for I have seen the worst, in my judgement, beforehand, and wors then y[t] can not bee."

"If the Queene pai not her souldiours she must loos her garrisons; ther is no dout thereof; but no man living shall be hable to sai the fault is in me. What releefe I can do them, I will. I will spare no danger, if occasion serves. I am sure no creature shall be hable to lay injustice to my charge; and, for furdre doutes, truly I stand not uppon them. We shall have a sore warr upon us this sommer, wherein if appointment had been kept, and these disgraces forborn, w[ch] have greatly weakened us, we had been victorious.—It hath been a costly beginning unto me this war, by reason I had nothing proportioned unto it; my servantes unexperienced, and myself every way unfurnished. . . . . . I have been vyldli deceaved for armures or horsemen; if yow cold speedily spare me any out of your armury, I will send them yow back as soon as my own be finished. There was never so good father find a more troublesome son." Dated at Utrecht, March 24.

The Belgians fought as men fight for liberty and life; the English, as loyal subjects and earnest allies; but the contest was unequal, and its progress discouraging and slow. The Spaniards were better trained, more subtle, and moreover inspired by the acute science and cool daring of the greatest general of the age. Alexander of Parma was the nephew, the rival, and the successor of Don John; possessing his ambition without his romance, his bravery, but not his fascination; inferior in the graces that woo and win; superior in military command, and in patient, unscrupulous execution. When but six years old, he had delightedly witnessed the siege of his native city, and its brave defence by his father, Ottavio Farnese. At eleven, he plead with tears for permission to serve as a volunteer at the battle of St. Quentin. In early manhood, in default of the excitements of war, he nightly perambulated the streets of Parma in disguise, to measure his sword with chance combatants who seemed worthy of his challenge. When the last crusade was proclaimed against the Turks, he flew to the Levant, obtained a place in the very front of the battle at Lepanto, sprang alone on board the doubly-armed treasure-ship of the enemy, cut a passage for his followers with superhuman strokes from his two-handed sword, and securing that galley, and another which was sent to its rescue, divided the immense booty between himself and his crew.* In the Netherlands, he won the battle of Gemblours by a desperate manœuvre, and showed himself equally ready for stratagem and for conflict. His stately demeanor, dark piercing eyes, fine features, and martial figure, habited in high ruff, gold-inlaid armor, and the decoration of the Golden Fleece, betokened the warrior and the prince. Self-poised, politic, and prudent, his very lenity towards the vanquished made him a more formidable foe than any of Philip's emissaries by whom he had been preceded.

Within a few months after the arrival of the English reinforcements, he besieged the towns of Grave, Venlo, and Nuys, all of which were compelled to surrender. The allied forces were less successful in their retaliation upon several

* Motley's Dutch Republic.

places in his possession. As Sidney's name is not mentioned in connection with these events, we infer that he was engaged elsewhere. In the month of June, however, in concert with the young Prince Maurice, of Nassau, he took the town of Axell, by a well-conducted surprise, and his discretion on that occasion furnishes an evidence of what he might have achieved as a military commander, had his life been spared. Previous to the attack, he drew up his soldiers in battle array, and addressed them in a strain of eloquence which, says the enthusiastic chronicler, "did so link their minds that they did desire rather to die in that service than to live in the contrary." He appealed to their Protestant zeal —for party fervor, it must be remembered, was then religious, as well as military and political— to their loyalty, as subjects of a mighty Queen, to their pride, as sons of a glorious land, to their bravery, as men unfearing, in a noble cause, both danger and death.

The attack was made under the protecting darkness of night, and Sir Philip, with a tact that reminds us of a Scipio or a Polybius, revived the discipline of the Roman legion.

In silence and order the little band marched, unheard, to the very walls of Axell, and scaled them by ladders, without the loss of a single man;

and while a chosen phalanx planted itself in the broad market square, the rest secured the garrison, and took possession of the public buildings. When the service was achieved, Sir Philip liberally rewarded them from his private purse.*

About this time the Duke of Parma laid siege to Rhineberg, an important post which the States were extremely solicitous to retain. Leicester determined at last upon some decisive stroke which should satisfy his confederates; but, not venturing with his inferior numbers upon an engagement, he directed his forces to the assault of Zutphen, a strong town in Guelderland, whose resistance to the Duke of Alba, fourteen years before, had been avenged by the command to his soldiery not to leave a man alive, or a single house unburned. The horrors that followed this atrocious order seem incredible, even in the annals of that sanguinary day. The garrison were put to the sword without a moment's warning, and life was wellnigh extinguished in the city.

* Fulke Greville's Life of Sir Philip Sidney. It appears from letters found in Wright's and Ellis's Collections that Sir Philip's munificence sometimes occasioned him serious embarrassment. He complains to Hatton, in 1581, of being deeply involved in debt, and, after his death, Walsingham wrote to Leicester that he must pay £6000 on his account, adding, however, "I weigh it nothing in respect of the loss of the gentleman who was my chiefe worldly comforte."

Five hundred burghers were tied together in pairs, and drowned in the river Yssel; the fugitives were caught and hung upon the gallows, until released by death from their tortures. And though the wail of agony, "a sound as of a mighty massacre," was heard far beyond the city, the terrified listeners dared not approach for days after its doom was sealed.*

The English troops, comprising 7000 foot and 1400 dragoons, encamped before Zutphen, in the month of September, having first obtained possession of the little town of Doesberg, seven miles distant. The Governor had sent word to the Duke of Parma of his inability to sustain a siege, from the want of both provisions and ammunition. Had Leicester immediately secured certain passes by which the city was entered, it must of necessity have surrendered; but here was another proof of the military incapacity which marked this whole campaign. Parma hastily raised the siege of Rhineberg, and marched his forces to the relief of Zutphen; sending in advance the Italian cavalry, under the Marquis del Guasto, with temporary supplies. On the night of the 21st, a portion of them were conveyed without difficulty into the town, and, though the dawn broke before

* Motley's Dutch Republic.

the labor was completed, the Marquis resolved to hazard its continuance.

It was a chill, gray morning. The fog rolled heavily up from the banks of the Yssel, and flung its spectral mantle over the beleaguered city and the white tents of the besiegers.

"Their camp lay on the shadowy hill, all silent as a cloud;
Its very heart of life stood still—and the white mist brought
its shroud;
For Death was walking in the dark, and grimly smiled to see
How all was ranged and ready for his sumptuous jubilee." *

The Italian and Spanish cavalry, 3000 in number, conducted by Del Guasto and several distinguished officers, were suddenly encountered by 500 of the English cavalry,† under the command of Sir Philip Sidney and Sir John Norris. The former were driven back by a furious onset, but rallying to the charge, a combat ensued so ardent and impetuous on both sides, that its very name was long after a proverb in the land. Robert

* Gerald Massey.

† This is Stowe's account, but in the "Histoire des Provinces Unies, par Leclerc," tome i. p. 128, we are told that the English numbered 1500 infantry and 200 cavalry.

A full narration of this engagement is also found in the "Historische Beschreibung dess Niederlandischen Kriegs; vom Jahr 1560 biss auff 1620, durch Emanuel von Meteren. Amsterdam 1627," page 531.

Sidney performed such prodigies of valor that he was knighted on the field; Sir William Russel charged so terribly with spear and curtelax that "the enemy reported him to be a devil and not a man;" young Essex shouted, as he threw his lance upon the first assailant, "For the honor of England, my fellows, follow me!" Lord Willoughby, Lord North, and many others, earned great distinction. But foremost in the hot affray, where loudest rang the clash of steel and deadly fire of arquebuse and musket, wherever the wounded fell, the timorous faltered, or the hostile host was fiercest, there glittered the gilded armor of our gallant Sidney—as he spurred his white charger through the storm of bullets, now to encounter a fiery foe, anon to save a friend imperilled by unequal numbers. Two horses were shot beneath him, and he quickly mounted a third. Just as the Spanish cavalry were giving way, he saw Lord Willoughby surrounded by the enemy, and in imminent danger. Dashing over the prostrate slain—he rescued his friend, but was himself struck by a musket-ball which entered the left thigh, a little above the knee, dreadfully fracturing the bone, and riving the muscles far upward toward the body.* He was

* It is said that he had left the camp in full armor, but meeting the Marshal lightly armed, had divested himself of

instantly borne from the fatal spot, and a messenger carried the sad tidings to Lord Leicester. Men who had that day encountered the King of Terrors with undaunted eye, wept as they heard that the price of victory must be the death of Sidney. "O Philip!" cried the Earl, in the touching plaint of grief, "*I am sorry for thy hurt!*" "This have I done," replied the wounded hero, "to do you honor, and Her Majesty service." In death, as in life, he served, not himself, but his country and his friends. With tears of sorrow, Sir William Russel kissed his hand and said, "O noble Sir Philip, there was never any man attained hurt more honorably than you have done, or any served like unto you."

And here we have arrived at one of the last and most beautiful acts of a beautiful career. We record once more the story which has floated down on the echoing voices of almost three hundred years, and with its sweet lesson still thrills the soul of childhood and quickens the pulse of age. As he was borne from the field of action, faint, pallid, and parched with the thirst that attends excessive loss of blood, Sidney asked for water. It was obtained, doubtless, with difficulty

his greaves; an act, which some of his biographers consider a proof of courage, and others have censured for its indiscretion.

and in scant supply. With trembling hand he raised the cup to his lips, when his eye was arrested by the gaze of a dying soldier, longingly fixed upon the precious draught. Without tasting, he instantly handed it to the sufferer, with the memorable words, "*Thy necessity is greater than mine!*" *

The affection of Leicester for his nephew was

* This incident was the subject of a painting by Benjamin West, a description of which, taken from Zouch's Life of Sidney, we here insert:

"The centre of this composition is occupied by the wounded hero, Sir Philip Sidney, seated on a litter, who, while his wound is dressing by the attending surgeons, is ordering the water (which is pouring out for him to allay the extreme thirst he suffered from the loss of blood) to be given to a wounded soldier, to whom he points, in the second group to his right, who had cast a longing look toward it. Behind, and to the left of Sidney, the Earl of Leicester, in dark armor, is discovered as commander in chief, issuing his orders to the surrounding cavalry, as engaged in the confusion of the contending armies. Among the several spirited war-horses that are introduced, that of Sidney, a white horse, is seen under the management of his servant, but still restive and ungovernable. The portrait of the artist is found to the right of the picture, the figure leaning on a horse in the foreground, and contemplating the interesting scene before him. The background, and to the extreme distance of the horizon, the movements of the armies, and the rage of battle are everywhere visible, enveloped in an atmosphere that has fixed upon it the true aspect of danger and dismay."

the redeeming point in his character. In the simple language of sincere distress, he wrote, the day after the battle :—

" This young manne, he was my greatest comforte, next her Majestie, of all the worlde, and if I could buy his lieffe, with all I have, to my sherte, I would give yt. How God will dispose of him I know not, but feare I must needes greatly the worste ; the blow in so dangerous a place and so great; yet did I never hear of any manne that did abide the dressinge and settinge of his bones better than he did. And he was carried afterwards in my barge to Arnheim, and I heare this day he ys still of good hearte, and comforteth all aboute him as much as may be. God of his mercie graunt me his lieffe, which I cannot but doubt of greatly. I was abrode that time in the fielde, givinge some order to supplie that business, which did indure almost twoe owres in continuall fighte, and meetinge Philip commynge on horsebacke, not a little to my greafe.—Well, I praye God, yf it be his will, save me his lieffe ; even as well for her Majestie's service sake, as for myne own comforte."

The utmost art of the imperfect surgery of the time was bestowed upon the illustrious patient, and the devoted care of Lady Sidney and several friends attended him during the sixteen days that intervened until his death. Hopes of his recovery were at first encouraged, but the bullet, which was supposed to have been poisoned, could not be extracted. The solicitous inquiries that were constantly sent from both Belgium and England, proved, if proof were needed, how highly his life was prized; and Count Hohenlo exclaimed with the blunt fervor of a soldier to the surgeon who expressed his apprehension of a fatal result, "Away, villain, never see my face again, till thou bring better news of that man's recovery, for whose redemption many such as I were happily lost."

Sir Philip seems to have been visited from the first with premonitions of his death; but the messenger from the spirit land came to him, not as a spectre of fear, but as an angel of hope. Through suffering so extreme that even the bones of the shoulder were worn through the skin, he was patient, placid, and loving; so tranquil, indeed, that he wrote a long letter to an eminent divine in pure and elegant Latin, composed an ode, (unfortunately not preserved,) on the approach of dissolution, discoursed at length and with argumentative clearness on the immortality of the soul, and dictated his will with minute remembrance of all his friends and servants.*

* Of that instrument Sir Fulke Greville says, "This will of

With the undoubting confidence of religious faith, he imputed the fatal disaster, not to chance, but to the immediate ordinance of the Creator; and not only expressed entire resignation, but even avowed himself grateful for sufferings "which should profit him whether he lived or died." "Love my memory," said he to his afflicted brother, "cherish my friends; their faith to me may assure you that they are honest. But, above all, govern your will and affections by the will and word of your Creator, in me beholding the end of this world with all its vanities."

There is a simple and touching little sketch of his last illness, written by his chaplain, who was his constant attendant during its continuance. It is still preserved in the British Museum, and quoted at length by Dr. Zouch, and we are confident that a few brief extracts cannot fail to be of interest:—

"The night before he died, towards the morning, I asked him how he did. He answered, 'I feel myself more weak.' 'I trust,' said I, 'you are well, and thoroughly prepared for death, yf

his will ever remain for a witness to the world that, even dying, those sweet and large affections in him could no more be contracted with the narrowness of pain, grief, or sickness, than any sparkle of our immortality can be privately buried in the shadows of death."

God shall call you.' At this he made a little pause, and then he answered, 'I have a doubt; pray resolve me in it. I have not slept this night; I have verie earnestlie and humblie besought the Lord to give me some sleep; he hath denied it; this causeth me to doubt that God doth not regard me, nor heare any of my prayers; this doth trouble me.' Answer was made that, for matters touching salvation or pardon of our sins through Christ, he gave an absolute promise; but, for things concerning this life, God hath promised them but with caution; that which he hath absolutely promised we may assuredly look to receive, craving in faith that which he hath thus promised. 'I am,' said he, 'fully satisfied, and resolved with this answer. No doubt it is even so; then I will submit myself to his will in these outward things.' He added, farther, 'I had this night a trouble in my mynd; for, searching myself, methought I had not a full and sure hould of Christ. After I had continued in this perplexity awhile, how strangelie God did deliver me! There came to my remembrance a vanity in which I delighted, whereof I had not rid myself. I rid myself of it, and presently my joie and comfort returned.'—Within a few hours after, I told him that I thought his death did approach, which indeed he well perceived, and for which he prepared himself. His fear that death would take away his understanding did continue. 'I doe,' said he, 'with trembling hart, most humblie intreat the Lord that the pangs of death may not be so grievous as to take away my understanding.'

"It was proved to him by testimonies and infallible reasons out of the Scriptures, that, although his understanding and senses should fail, yet that faith, which he had now, could not fail, but would hold still the power and victory before God. At this, he did with a chearful and smiling countenance put forth his hand, and slappt me softlie on the cheeks. Not long after, he lifted up his eyes and hands, uttering these words, '*I would not chaunge my joye for the empire of the worlde;*' for the nearer he saw death approach, the more his comfort seemed to increase.—As the light of a lamp is continued by pouring in of oyl, so he sought to have the burning zeal and flame of his prayer, upon which his heart was still bent, cherished by the comforts of the holy word; accounting it a great injury, if we did not seek to give wings to his faith to carry up his prayers speedily, uttering grief when he felt any thought interrupting him.

"Having made a comparison of God's grace now in him, his former virtues seemed to be nothing; for he wholly condemned his former life. 'All things in it,' said he, 'have been vaine, vaine, vaine.'

"It now seemed as if all natural heat and life were almost utterly gone out of him, that his understanding had failed, and that it was to no purpose to speak any more unto him. But it was far otherwise. I spake thus unto him: 'Sir, if you heare what I saye, let us by some means know it, and if you have still your inward joye and consolation in God, hould up your hand.' With that, he did lift up his hand, and stretched it forth on high, which we thought he could scarce have moved, and it caused the beholders to cry out with joy, that his understanding should be still so perfect, and that the weak body, beyond all expectation, should so readily give a sign of the joye of the soul. After this, asking him to lift up his hands to God, seeing he could not speak or open his eyes—that we might see his heart still prayed, he raised both his hands, and set them together on his breast, and held them upwards, after the manner of those which make humble petitions; and so his hands did remain, and even so stiff, that they would have so continued standing, but that we took the one from the other."

A little before his death, he called for music; and thus, amid the harmonies of earth, the benedictions of love, and the incense of prayer, the spirit of Philip Sidney soared to the spheres of Mystery and of Promise.

It was on the 17th day of October, and his age was nearly thirty-two. In life, the patriot, the scholar, the pride of chivalry; in death, the hero, the philosopher, and the Christian.

When a nation weeps, the sorrow is sincere, the tribute is sublime. England bewailed, with almost unprecedented sorrow, the loss of her most promising son. The higher ranks all assumed the garb of mourning, and for many months no one, at Court or in the city, appeared in gay attire,—an honor never before accorded to a private individual. The Queen expressed the deepest sorrow. Lord Buckhurst wrote to Leicester, "By the decease of that noble gentleman, her Majesty and the whole realm do suffer no small loss and detriment. He hath had as great love in this life, and as many tears for his death, as ever any had." Du Plessis said to Walsingham, "I have experienced troubles and disappointments in these troublous times, but nothing which lay heavier upon me, nor so struck me to the heart, no private or public calamity which ever so sensibly affected me. I bewail his loss, and regret him, not for England only; but for all Christendom."

Even the flinty heart of Philip II. was softened for an instant, as he prophetically exclaimed, "England has lost in one moment what she may not produce in an age;" and his secretary, Mendoza, remarked that, "however glad he was his master had lost an enemy, yet he could not but lament to see Christendom deprived of so rare a light in those cloudy times." The United Provinces besought the privilege of his burial, promising to raise "as fair a monument as had any prince in Europe, yea, though it should cost half a ton of gold." The Queen refused the request, preferring to honor the memory of her knight by assuming, herself, the expenses of a magnificent funeral. With solemn pomp his remains were removed to Flushing, and thence embarked for England. The English garrison, twelve hundred in number, headed the procession, marching by three and three, their halberts, pikes, and ensigns trailing on the ground. Next came the coffin covered with a pall of velvet, then the burghers of the town in deep mourning, slowly and sadly marching to the sound of muffled drums and softly breathing fifes. A triple volley of small shot was fired, followed by two discharges from the great ordnance about the walls. "And so," says the Chronicle, "they took their leave of their well-beloved governor." His honored relics were transported in a pinnace of his own, whose "sayles, tackling, and other furniture were coloured blacke, and blacke clothe hung round her with escuchions of his arms, and she was accompanied with divers other shipps." The body lay in state at Aldgate until the 16th of February, when it was deposited in St. Paul's Cathedral, with a splendor of ceremonial unparalleled, except for royalty. The Lord Mayor and the Aldermen on horseback, in their scarlet gowns lined with ermine, seven representatives of the seven United Provinces clothed in black, several companies with their insignia, and a very numerous train of citizens, poured the tide of mournful homage through the streets of London. The pall was supported by the Earls of Huntingdon, Essex, Leicester, and Pembroke, and the Barons Willoughby and North. Sir Robert Sidney was chief mourner, his parents having both died a few months after Sir Philip was sent to Holland.*

Upon a pillar in the choir of St. Paul's, there

* Sir Philip left one child, a daughter, named Elizabeth, who was said to inherit much of her father's character. She married Roger Manners, fifth Earl of Rutland, and died without children. Lady Sidney married three years after her husband's death, the Earl of Essex, and subsequently, the Earl of Clanrickard.

formerly hung a tablet, graven with the following epitaph, which, it is now believed. was written by Sir Walter Raleigh :—

> " England, Netherlands, the heavens, and the arts,
> The soldier, and the world, have made six parts
> Of the noble Sidney, for none will suppose
> That a small heap of stones can Sidney inclose
> His body hath England, for she it bred,
> Netherlands, his blood, in her defence shed ;
> The heavens have his soul, the arts have his fame,
> All soldier's the grief, and the world, his good name."

The Universities of Cambridge and Oxford expressed, in three volumes of adulatory Greek and Latin verse, their esteem and sorrow. An elegiac plaint from James of Scotland, swelled the voice of universal praise ; and, it is said, that more than two hundred noted writers have, at different times, borne testimony to his merits. Camden wrote of him :—

" This is that Sidney, whom, as Providence seems to have sent into the world to give the present age a specimen of the antients, so did it on a sudden recall him, and snatch him from us, as more worthy of heaven than of earth. Thus, when virtue is come to perfection, it presently leaves us, and the best things are seldom lasting. Rest, then, in peace, O Sidney, if I may be allowed this address. We will not celebrate thy memory with tears, but with admiration. Whatever we loved in thee, (as the best author speaks of the best governor of Britain,) whatever we admired in thee continues, and will continue, in the memories of men, the revolutions of ages, and the annals of time. Many, as inglorious and ignoble, are buried in oblivion, but Sidney shall live to all posterity. For, as the Greek poet has it, Virtue's beyond the reach of Fate."

Spenser commemorated his patron under his poetical appellation of Astrophel, and also in two Epitaphs, which contain these lines:—

"A King gave thee thy name; a Kingly minde
That God thee gave, who found it now too deere
For this base world, and hath resumde it neere,
To sit in skies, and sort with powers divine.
Kent thy birth-daies, and Oxford held thy youth;
The heavens made haste, and staid nor years nor time;
The fruits of age grew ripe in thy first prime,
Thy will, thy words; thy words the seales of truth.
Great gifts and wisdom rare imployd thee thence,
To treat from Kings with those more great than Kings;
Such hope men had to lay the highest things
On thy wise youth, to be transported thence!

* * * * * * *

What hath he lost, that such great grace hath won?
Young years for endless years, and hope unsure
Of fortune's gifts, for wealth that still shall dure;
Oh! happy race with so great praises run!"

18 *

Thomson has enshrined the memory of Sir Philip, in his harmonious verse:—

> "Nor can the Muse the gallant Sidney pass,
> The plume of war! with early laurels crowned,
> The lover's myrtle, and the poet's bay."

Campbell bestowed a tribute of united praise upon Sidney and Spenser:—

> "The man that looks sweet Sidney in the face,
> Beholding there love's truest majesty,
> And the soft image of departed grace,
> Shall fill his mind with magnanimity;
> There may he read unfeigned humility,
> And golden pity, born of heavenly flood,
> Unsullied thought of immortality,
> And musing virtue, prodigal of blood;
> Yes, in this map of what is fair and good,
> This glorious index of a heavenly book,
> Not seldom, as in youthful years he stood,
> Divinest Spenser would admiring look,
> And framing thence high wit and pure desire,
> Imagined deeds that set the world on fire."

"Sidney trod," says the author of the Effigiæ Poeticæ, "from his cradle to his grave, amid incense and flowers, and died in a dream of glory."

It is needless to dilate upon the talents and the virtues of Philip Sidney; equally needless, and more perplexing, to attempt further selection from the oblations that have been profusely thrown upon his shrine. By the consenting acclaim of all his contemporaries, by the impartial voice of succeeding ages, even by the critical fiat of the nineteenth century, he stands in the Pantheon of Fame. But to the world at large, he stands there rather as a luminous, half-defined phantom, than as a sculptured form; and many marvel that a man whose years were few, whose achievements were of no startling greatness, whose words created no era in thought, is encircled with a halo, which neither melts before Time, nor is dimmed by a brightening civilization. We believe that the solution is twofold. In the first place, he was the representative of the finest features of his country and his age. Under happy coincidences of nature and of education, he embodied and idealized the patriotism, the piety, the intellectual activity, the practical energy, and the romantic knight-errantry, for which Europe, and especially England, was at that time distinguished. He seemed, besides, to be a connecting link between the ancient cavalier and the modern gentleman, blending in focal beauty the martial valor, the ceremonious courtesy, the religious devotion of the one, with the culture, the refinements, and the lofty independence of the other.

The prestige that attends him is farther heightened by the harmony of his social and spiritual nature. It is the homage that mankind universally pays to that consistent goodness, which, emanating from an aspiring, well-balanced soul, atmospheres the life with depths as pellucid and serene as those of an Egyptian sky. We view his character from every side with satisfaction; and so perfect are its proportions, that we forget their individual dignity, in admiration of their concentred beauty. Generous and genial, possessing an inherent nobility that lifted him far above the littleness of envy and deceit, his common and daily acts impressed men with his sincerity and his justice. His conversation and his writings not only revealed the affluence of a well-stored mind, they were the lofty utterances of one who dwelt amid the Alpine peaks of thought. The heroism, the purity, the spiritual beauty that he portrayed, were the echoes of a soul that answered but to the inspiration of Truth. Even his fault—we are constrained to use the singular—that of a somewhat impetuous temper, was the mere effervescence of an intense nature, and scarcely detracted from his essential consistency.

> " We should count time by heart-throbs,
> Not by hours upon a dial. He most lives,
> Who thinks most, feels the noblest, acts the best."

Though his life was undistinguished by action,

it glowed with all the elements of greatness. In his embassy to Germany, in his letter to the Queen, in his conduct in Belgium, and on the field of Zutphen, we see the germ of powers that needed but time and occasion for an unfolding, that would have ranked him with the wisest of statesmen, the most renowned of soldiers. Nevertheless, it is by the attraction of character, rather than by the grandeur of deeds, or the splendor of genius, that the fame of Philip Sidney retains its vitality. No hours of indolence or of folly left their blank record upon his tomb; the daily and hourly culture of taste, of knowledge, and of virtue graved the moral of a life which, though brief in years, was fruitful in those results which give to life at once its beauty and its reward.

THE END.

☞ Any Books in this list will be sent free of postage, on receipt of price.

Boston, 135 Washington Street,
October, 1860.

A LIST OF BOOKS

PUBLISHED BY

TICKNOR AND FIELDS.

Sir Walter Scott.

Illustrated Household Edition of the Waverley Novels. In portable size, 16mo. form. Now Complete. Price 75 cents a volume.

The paper is of fine quality; the stereotype plates are not old ones repaired, the type having been cast expressly for this edition. The Novels are illustrated with capital steel plates engraved in the best manner, after drawings and paintings by the most eminent artists, among whom are Birket Foster, Darley, Billings, Landseer, Harvey, and Faed. This Edition contains all the latest notes and corrections of the author, a Glossary and Index; and some curious additions, especially in "Guy Mannering" and the "Bride of Lammermoor;" being the fullest edition of the Novels ever published. *The notes are at the foot of the page,*—a great convenience to the reader.

Any of the following Novels sold separate.

Waverley, 2 vols.	St. Ronan's Well, 2 vols.
Guy Mannering, 2 vols.	Redgauntlet, 2 vols.
The Antiquary, 2 vols.	The Betrothed, } 2 vols.
Rob Roy, 2 vols.	The Highland Widow, } 2 vols.
Old Mortality, 2 vols.	The Talisman, } 2 vols.
Black Dwarf, } 2 vols.	Two Drovers, } 2 vols.
Legend of Montrose, } 2 vols.	My Aunt Margaret's Mirror, } 2 vols.
Heart of Mid Lothian, 2 vols.	The Tapestried Chamber, } 2 vols.
Bride of Lammermoor, 2 vols.	The Laird's Jock. } 2 vols.
Ivanhoe, 2 vols.	Woodstock, 2 vols.
The Monastery, 2 vols.	The Fair Maid of Perth, 2 vols.
The Abbot, 2 vols.	Anne of Geierstein, 2 vols.
Kenilworth, 2 vols.	Count Robert of Paris, 2 vols.
The Pirate, 2 vols.	The Surgeon's Daughter, } 2 vols.
The Fortunes of Nigel, 2 vols.	Castle Dangerous, } 2 vols.
Peveril of the Peak, 2 vols.	Index and Glossary. } 2 vols.
Quentin Durward, 2 vols.	

Tales of a Grandfather. *In Press.*

Life. By J. G. Lockhart. *In Press.*

Thomas De Quincey.

CONFESSIONS OF AN ENGLISH OPIUM-EATER, AND SUSPIRIA DE PROFUNDIS. With Portrait. 75 cents.

BIOGRAPHICAL ESSAYS. 75 cents.

MISCELLANEOUS ESSAYS. 75 cents.

THE CÆSARS. 75 cents.

LITERARY REMINISCENCES. 2 vols. $1.50.

NARRATIVE AND MISCELLANEOUS PAPERS. 2 vols. $1.50.

ESSAYS ON THE POETS, &c. 1 vol. 16mo. 75 cents.

HISTORICAL AND CRITICAL ESSAYS. 2 vols. $1.50.

AUTOBIOGRAPHIC SKETCHES. 1 vol. 75 cents.

ESSAYS ON PHILOSOPHICAL WRITERS, &c. 2 vols. 16mo. $1.50.

LETTERS TO A YOUNG MAN, AND OTHER PAPERS. 1 vol. 75 cents.

THEOLOGICAL ESSAYS AND OTHER PAPERS. 2 vols. $1.50.

THE NOTE BOOK. 1 vol. 75 cents.

MEMORIALS AND OTHER PAPERS. 2 vols. 16mo. $1.50.

THE AVENGER AND OTHER PAPERS. 1 vol. 75 cents.

LOGIC OF POLITICAL ECONOMY, AND OTHER PAPERS. 1 vol. 75 cents.

Alfred Tennyson.

POETICAL WORKS. With Portrait. 2 vols. Cloth. $2.00.

POCKET EDITION OF POEMS COMPLETE. 75 cents.

THE PRINCESS. Cloth. 50 cents.

IN MEMORIAM. Cloth. 75 cents.

MAUD, AND OTHER POEMS. Cloth. 50 cents.

IDYLS OF THE KING. A new volume. Cloth. 75 cents.

Barry Cornwall.

ENGLISH SONGS AND OTHER SMALL POEMS. $1.00.

DRAMATIC POEMS. Just published. $1.00.

ESSAYS AND TALES IN PROSE. 2 vols. $1.50.

Henry W. Longfellow.

POETICAL WORKS. In two volumes. 16mo. Boards. $2.00.

POCKET EDITION OF POETICAL WORKS. In two volumes. $1.75.

POCKET EDITION OF PROSE WORKS COMPLETE. In two volumes. $1.75.

THE SONG OF HIAWATHA. $1.00.

EVANGELINE: A Tale of Acadia. 75 cents.

THE GOLDEN LEGEND. A Poem. $1.00.

HYPERION. A Romance. $1.00.

OUTRE-MER. A Pilgrimage. $1.00.

KAVANAGH. A Tale. 75 cents.

THE COURTSHIP OF MILES STANDISH. 1 vol. 16mo. 75 cents.

Illustrated editions of EVANGELINE. POEMS, HYPERION, THE GOLDEN LEGEND, and MILES STANDISH.

Charles Reade.

PEG WOFFINGTON. A Novel. 75 cents.

CHRISTIE JOHNSTONE. A Novel. 75 cents.

CLOUDS AND SUNSHINE. A Novel. 75 cents.

'NEVER TOO LATE TO MEND.' 2 vols. $1.50.

WHITE LIES. A Novel. 1 vol. $1.25.

PROPRIA QUÆ MARIBUS and THE BOX TUNNEL. 25 cts.

THE EIGHTH COMMANDMENT. 75 cents.

Thomas Hood.

MEMORIALS. Edited by his Children. 2 vols. $1.75.

James Russell Lowell.

COMPLETE POETICAL WORKS. In Blue and Gold. 2 vols. $1.50.

POETICAL WORKS. 2 vols. 16mo. Cloth. $1.50.

SIR LAUNFAL. New Edition. 25 cents.

A FABLE FOR CRITICS. New Edition. 50 cents.

THE BIGLOW PAPERS. A New Edition. 63 cents.

FIRESIDE TRAVELS. *In Press.*

Nathaniel Hawthorne.

Twice-Told Tales. Two volumes. $1.50.
The Scarlet Letter. 75 cents.
The House of the Seven Gables. $1.00.
The Snow Image, and other Tales. 75 cents.
The Blithedale Romance. 75 cents.
Mosses from an Old Manse. 2 vols. $1.50.
The Marble Faun. 2 vols. $1.50.
True Stories. 75 cents.
A Wonder-Book for Girls and Boys. 75 cents.
Tanglewood Tales. 88 cents.

William Howitt.

Land, Labor, and Gold. 2 vols. $2.00.
A Boy's Adventures in Australia. 75 cents.

Charles Kingsley.

Two Years Ago. A New Novel. $1.25.
Amyas Leigh. A Novel. $1.25.
Glaucus; or, the Wonders of the Shore. 50 cts.
Poetical Works. 75 cents.
The Heroes; or, Greek Fairy Tales. 75 cents.
Andromeda and other Poems. 50 cents.
Sir Walter Raleigh and his Time, &c. $1.25.
New Miscellanies. 1 vol. $1.00.

Coventry Patmore.

The Angel in the House. Betrothal.
" " " " Espousals. 75 cts. each.

George S. Hillard.

Six Months in Italy. 1 vol. 16mo. $1.50.
Dangers and Duties of the Mercantile Profession. 25 cents.
Selections from the Writings of Walter Savage Landor. 1 vol. 16mo. 75 cents.

Oliver Wendell Holmes.

POEMS. With fine Portrait. Cloth. $1.00.
ASTRÆA. Fancy paper. 25 cents.
THE AUTOCRAT OF THE BREAKFAST TABLE. With Illustrations by Hoppin. 16mo. $1.00.
The Same. Large Paper Edition. 8vo. Tinted paper. $3.00.
THE PROFESSOR AT THE BREAKFAST TABLE. 16mo. $1.00.
The Same. Large Paper Edition. 8vo. Tinted paper. $3.00.
POEMS. A new volume. *In Press.*
A VOLUME OF MEDICAL ESSAYS. *In Press.*

Ralph Waldo Emerson.

ESSAYS. 1st Series. 1 vol. $1.00.
ESSAYS. 2d Series. 1 vol. $1.00.
MISCELLANIES. 1 vol. $1.00.
REPRESENTATIVE MEN. 1 vol. $1.00.
ENGLISH TRAITS. 1 vol. $1.00.
POEMS. 1 vol. $1.00.
CONDUCT OF LIFE. 1 vol. $1.00. *Nearly ready.*

John G. Whittier.

POCKET EDITION OF POETICAL WORKS. 2 vols. $1.50.
OLD PORTRAITS AND MODERN SKETCHES. 75 cents.
MARGARET SMITH'S JOURNAL. 75 cents.
SONGS OF LABOR, AND OTHER POEMS. Boards. 50 cts.
THE CHAPEL OF THE HERMITS. Cloth. 50 cents.
LITERARY RECREATIONS, &c. Cloth. $1.00.
THE PANORAMA, AND OTHER POEMS. Cloth. 50 cents.
HOME BALLADS AND POEMS. 1 vol. 75 cents.

Edwin P. Whipple.

ESSAYS AND REVIEWS. 2 vols. $2.00.
LECTURES ON LITERATURE AND LIFE. 63 cents.
WASHINGTON AND THE REVOLUTION. 20 cents.

Robert Browning.

POETICAL WORKS. 2 vols. $2.00.

MEN AND WOMEN. 1 vol. $1.00.

Henry Giles.

LECTURES, ESSAYS, &c. 2 vols. $1.50.

DISCOURSES ON LIFE. 75 cents.

ILLUSTRATIONS OF GENIUS. Cloth. $1.00.

William Motherwell.

COMPLETE POETICAL WORKS. In Blue and Gold. 1 vol. 75 cents.

MINSTRELSY, ANC. AND MOD. 2 vols. Boards. $1.50.

Capt. Mayne Reid.

THE PLANT HUNTERS. With Plates. 75 cents.

THE DESERT HOME: OR, THE ADVENTURES OF A LOST FAMILY IN THE WILDERNESS. With fine Plates. $1.00.

THE BOY HUNTERS. With fine Plates. 75 cents.

THE YOUNG VOYAGEURS: OR, THE BOY HUNTERS IN THE NORTH. With Plates. 75 cents.

THE FOREST EXILES. With fine Plates. 75 cents.

THE BUSH BOYS. With fine Plates. 75 cents.

THE YOUNG YAGERS. With fine Plates. 75 cents.

RAN AWAY TO SEA: AN AUTOBIOGRAPHY FOR BOYS. With fine Plates. 75 cents.

THE BOY TAR: A VOYAGE IN THE DARK. A New Book. With fine Plates. 75 cents.

ODD PEOPLE. With Plates. *Nearly ready.*

THE BOY'S BOOK OF ANIMALS. With Plates. *In Press.*

Goethe.

WILHELM MEISTER. Translated by *Carlyle.* 2 vols. $2.50.

FAUST. Translated by *Hayward.* 75 cents.

FAUST. Translated by *Charles T. Brooks.* $1.00.

CORRESPONDENCE WITH A CHILD. *Bettina.* 1 vol. 12mo. $1.25.

J. G. Lockhart.

SPANISH BALLADS. With Portrait. 75 cents.

Rev. Charles Lowell.

PRACTICAL SERMONS. 1 vol. 12mo. $1.25.
OCCASIONAL SERMONS. With fine Portrait. $1.25.

Rev. F. W. Robertson.

SERMONS. First Series. $1.00.
" Second " $1.00.
" Third " $1.00.
" Fourth " $1.00.
LECTURES AND ADDRESSES ON LITERARY AND SOCIAL TOPICS. $1.00.

R. H. Stoddard.

POEMS. Cloth. 63 cents.
ADVENTURES IN FAIRY LAND. 75 cents.
SONGS OF SUMMER. 75 cents.

Anna Mary Howitt.

AN ART STUDENT IN MUNICH. $1.25.
A SCHOOL OF LIFE. A Story. 75 cents.

Mary Russell Mitford.

OUR VILLAGE. Illustrated. 2 vols. 16mo. $2.50.
ATHERTON, AND OTHER STORIES. 1 vol. 16mo. $1.25.

Mrs. Howe.

PASSION FLOWERS. 75 cents.
WORDS FOR THE HOUR. 75 cents.
THE WORLD'S OWN. 50 cents.
A TRIP TO CUBA. 1 vol. 16mo. 75 cents.

Grace Greenwood.

GREENWOOD LEAVES. 1st and 2d Series. $1.25 each.
POETICAL WORKS. With fine Portrait. 75 cents.
HISTORY OF MY PETS. With six fine Engravings. Scarlet cloth. 50 cents.
RECOLLECTIONS OF MY CHILDHOOD. With six fine Engravings. Scarlet cloth. 50 cents.
HAPS AND MISHAPS OF A TOUR IN EUROPE. $1.25.
MERRIE ENGLAND. 75 cents.
A FOREST TRAGEDY, AND OTHER TALES. $1.00.
STORIES AND LEGENDS. 75 cents.
STORIES FROM FAMOUS BALLADS. Illustrated. 50 cents.

Mrs. Crosland.

LYDIA: A WOMAN'S BOOK. Cloth. 75 cents.
ENGLISH TALES AND SKETCHES. Cloth. $1.00.
MEMORABLE WOMEN. Illustrated. $1.00.

Mrs. Jameson.

CHARACTERISTICS OF WOMEN.	Blue and	Gold.	75 cents.
LOVES OF THE POETS.	"	"	75 cents.
DIARY OF AN ENNUYÉE	"	"	75 cents.
SKETCHES OF ART, &c.	"	"	75 cents.
STUDIES AND STORIES.	"	"	75 cents.
ITALIAN PAINTERS.	"	"	75 cents.
LEGENDS OF THE MADONNA.	"	"	75 cents.

Mrs. Mowatt.

AUTOBIOGRAPHY OF AN ACTRESS. $1.25.
PLAYS. ARMAND AND FASHION. 50 cents.
MIMIC LIFE. 1 vol. $1.25.
THE TWIN ROSES. 1 vol. 75 cents.

Alice Cary.

POEMS. 1 vol. 16mo. $1.00.
CLOVERNOOK CHILDREN. With Plates. 75 cents.

Mrs. Eliza B. Lee.

MEMOIR OF THE BUCKMINSTERS. $1.25.

FLORENCE, THE PARISH ORPHAN. 50 cents.

PARTHENIA. 1 vol. 16mo. $1.00.

Samuel Smiles.

LIFE OF GEORGE STEPHENSON: ENGINEER. $1.00.

SELF HELP; WITH ILLUSTRATIONS OF CHARACTER AND CONDUCT. 1 vol. 75 cents.

BRIEF BIOGRAPHIES. With Plates. $1.25.

Blanchard Jerrold.

DOUGLAS JERROLD'S WIT. 75 cents.

LIFE AND LETTERS OF DOUGLAS JERROLD. $1.00.

Miss Cummins.

EL FUREIDIS. By the Author of "The Lamplighter," &c. $1.00.

Mrs. Judson.

ALDERBROOK. By *Fanny Forrester.* 2 vols. $1.75.

THE KATHAYAN SLAVE, AND OTHER PAPERS. 1 vol. 63 cents.

MY TWO SISTERS: A SKETCH FROM MEMORY. 50 cents.

John G. Saxe.

POEMS. With Portrait. Boards. 63 cents. Cloth. 75 cents.

THE MONEY KING, AND OTHER POEMS. 1 vol. 75 cents.

Charles T. Brooks.

GERMAN LYRICS. Translated. 1 vol. 16mo. Cloth. $1.00.

Leigh Hunt.

POEMS. Blue and Gold. 2 vols. $1.50.

Tom Brown.

SCHOOL DAYS AT RUGBY. By *An Old Boy.* 1 vol. 16mo. $1.00.

The Same. Illustrated edition. $1.50.

THE SCOURING OF THE WHITE HORSE, OR THE LONG VACATION HOLIDAY OF A LONDON CLERK. By *The Author of 'School Days at Rugby.'* 1 vol. 16mo. $1.00.

TOM BROWN AT OXFORD. A Sequel to School Days at Rugby. Parts I to VIII. 12 cents each.

Gerald Massey.

POETICAL WORKS. Blue and Gold. 75 cents.

W. M. Thackeray.

BALLADS. 1 vol. 16mo. 75 cents.

Charles Mackay.

POEMS. 1 vol. Cloth. $1.00.

George H. Boker.

PLAYS AND POEMS. 2 vols. $2.00.

Henry T. Tuckerman.

POEMS. Cloth. 75 cents.

James G. Percival.

POETICAL WORKS. 2 vols. Blue and Gold. $1.75.

Arthur P. Stanley.

LIFE AND CORRESPONDENCE OF DR. ARNOLD. With fine Portrait. 2 vols. $2.00.

Henry Kingsley.

RECOLLECTIONS OF GEOFFRY HAMLYN. A Novel. $1.25.

Theophilus Parsons.

A MEMOIR OF CHIEF JUSTICE THEOPHILUS PARSONS, WITH NOTICES OF SOME OF HIS CONTEMPORARIES. By his Son. With Portrait. 1 vol. 12mo. $1.50.

Alexander Smith.

A LIFE DRAMA. 1 vol. 16mo. 50 cents.
CITY POEMS. With Portrait. 1 vol. 16mo. 63 cents.

Bayard Taylor.

POEMS OF HOME AND TRAVEL. Cloth. 75 cents.
POEMS OF THE ORIENT. Cloth. 75 cents.

Horace Mann.

THOUGHTS FOR A YOUNG MAN. 25 cents.

Lord Dufferin.

A YACHT VOYAGE OF 6,000 MILES. $1.00.

Owen Meredith.

POETICAL WORKS. Blue and Gold. 75 cents.
LUCILE: A Poem. Blue and Gold. 75 cents.

T. B. Read.

POETICAL WORKS. 2 vols. $2.00.

Arago.

BIOGRAPHIES OF DISTINGUISHED SCIENTIFIC MEN. 16mo. 2 vols. $2.00.

John Neal.

TRUE WOMANHOOD. A Novel. 1 vol. $1.25.

Hans Christian Andersen.

THE SAND-HILLS OF JUTLAND. 1 vol. 16mo. 75 cents.

R. H. Dana, Jr.

To Cuba and Back, a Vacation Voyage, by the Author of "Two Years before the Mast." 75 cents.

George B. Prescott.

History, Theory and Practice of the Electric Telegraph. With 100 Illustrations. 1 vol. 12mo. $1.75.

Captain McClintock.

Narrative of the Voyage in search of Sir John Franklin and the Discovery of his Remains. With Maps and Illustrations. 1 vol. large 12mo. $1.50.

The Same. Cheaper Edition. With the same Maps and Illustrations. 75 cents.

Charles Eliot Norton.

Notes of Travel and Study in Italy. 1 vol. 16mo. $1.00.

Charles Robert Leslie, R. A.

Autobiographical Recollections. Edited by Tom Taylor. With Portrait. 1 vol. 12mo. $1.25.

Wild Sports of India. 75 cents.

Lake House. By Fanny Lewald. 75 cents.

Charles Sumner's Orations. 2 vols. $2.50.

Tyndall's Glaciers of the Alps. Illustrated. 1 vol. $1.50.

Travels, Researches, and Missionary Labors in Eastern Africa. By Dr. J. Lewis Krapf. 1 vol. With Map. $1.25.

Lyteria: A Dramatic Poem. By Josiah Phillips Quincy. 50 cents.

Charicles: A Dramatic Poem. By Josiah Phillips Quincy. 50 cents.

Poems. By Thomas W. Parsons. $1.00.

RECOLLECTIONS OF SHELLEY AND BYRON. By E. J. Trelawny. 75 cents.

LIGHT ON THE DARK RIVER: OR, MEMOIRS OF MRS. HAMLIN. By Mrs. Lawrence. 1 vol. 16mo. Cloth. $1.00.

THE LIFE AND WORKS OF GOETHE. By G. H. Lewes. 2 vols. 16mo. $2.50.

HOLMBY HOUSE: A TALE OF OLD NORTHAMPTONSHIRE. By G. J. Whyte Melville. 8vo. Paper. 50 cents.

MADEMOISELLE MORI: A TALE OF MODERN ROME. 1 vol. $1.25.

THE SEMI-DETACHED HOUSE. Edited by Lady Theresa Lewis. 1 vol. 75 cents.

FRESH HEARTS THAT FAILED THREE THOUSAND YEARS AGO. With other Poems. By the Author of "The New Priest in Conception Bay." 1 vol. 50 cents.

POEMS. By Miss Muloch, Author of "John Halifax," &c. 1 vol. 75 cents.

GUESSES AT TRUTH. 1 vol. 12mo.

ARABIAN DAYS' ENTERTAINMENTS. Translated from the German of W. Hauff. By H. Pelham Curtis. With Illustrations by Hoppin. 1 vol. $1.25.

HYMNS OF THE AGES. With a Preface by Rev. F. D. Huntington, D. D. 1 vol. 12mo. $1.00.

Also a fine Edition, on large paper. 8vo. Bevelled boards. $3.00.

THE CRUSADES AND THE CRUSADERS. By J. G. Edgar. With Illustrations. 75 cents.

ERNEST BRACEBRIDGE; OR, SCHOOLBOY DAYS. By W. H. G. Kingston. With Illustrations. 75 cents.

SWORD AND GOWN. By the Author of "Guy Livingstone." 1 vol. 75 cents.

ALMOST A HEROINE. By the Author of "Charles Auchester," and "Counterparts." 1 vol. $1.00.

RAB AND HIS FRIENDS. By John Brown, M. D. 15 cents.

TWELVE YEARS OF A SOLDIER'S LIFE: A MEMOIR OF THE LATE MAJOR W. S. R. HODSON, B. A. Edited by his Brother, Rev. George H. Hodson. 1 vol. $1.00.

THE LIFE AND TIMES OF SIR PHILIP SIDNEY. 1 vol. 16mo. $1.00.

Ernest Carroll, or Artist Life in Italy. 1 vol. 16mo. 88 cents.

Memory and Hope. Cloth. $2.00.

Thalatta: A Book for the Seaside. 75 cents.

Rejected Addresses. A new edition. Cloth. 75 cents.

Warreniana: A Companion to Rejected Addresses. 63 cents.

Angel Voices. 38 cents.

The Boston Book. $1.25.

Memoir of Robert Wheaton. 1 vol. $1.00.

Labor and Love: A Tale of English Life. 50 cts.

The Solitary of Juan Fernandez. By the Author of Picciola. 50 cents.

Walden: or, Life in the Woods. By Henry D. Thoreau. 1 vol. 16mo. $1.00.

Village Life in Egypt. By Bayle St. John, the Author of "Purple Tints of Paris." 2 vols. 16mo. $1.25.

Wensley: A Story without a Moral. By Edmund Quincy. 75 cents.

Palissy the Potter. By Henry Morley. 2 vols. 16mo. $1.50.

J. T. Buckingham's Personal Memoirs. 2 vols. $1.50.

The Barclays of Boston. By Mrs. H. G. Otis. 1 vol. 12mo. $1.25.

Sir Roger de Coverley. By Addison. From the "Spectator." 75 cents.

Sermons of Consolation. By F. W. P. Greenwood. $1.00.

Spain, her Institutions, Politics, and Public Men. By S. T. Wallis. $1.00.

Poems. By Henry Alford. $1.25.

Essays on the Formation of Opinions and the Pursuit of Truth. By Samuel Bailey. 1 vol. 16mo. $1.00.

Poems of Many Years. By Richard Monckton Milnes. Boards. 75 cents.

Bothwell. By W. Edmondstoune Aytoun. 75 cents.

Thorpe: A Quiet English Town, and Human Life therein. By William Mountford. 16mo. $1.00.

LECTURES ON ORATORY AND RHETORIC. By Prof. E. T. Channing. 75 cents.

A PHYSIOLOGICAL COOKERY BOOK. By Mrs. Horace Mann. 63 cents.

WILLIAM WORDSWORTH'S BIOGRAPHY. By Christopher Wosrdworth. 2 vols. $2.50.

NOTES FROM LIFE. By the Author of "Philip Van Artevelde." 1 vol. 16mo. Cloth. 63 cents.

ART OF PROLONGING LIFE. By Hufeland. Edited by Erasmus Wilson. 1 vol. 16mo. 75 cents.

SHELLEY MEMORIALS. From Authentic Sources. 1 vol. Cloth. 75 cents.

THORNDALE, OR THE CONFLICT OF OPINIONS. By William Smith. $1.25.

JOHN C. FREMONT'S LIFE, EXPLORATIONS, &c. By C. W. Upham. With Illustrations. 75 cents.

MONALDI: A Tale. By Washington Allston. 1 vol. 16mo. 75 cents.

HINTS ON HEALTH. By Dr. William E. Coale. 3d Edition. 63 cents.

SEVEN YEARS. A Volume of Stories. By Julia Kavanagh. 8vo. Paper, 30 cents.

POEMS. By Mrs. Rosa V. Johnson. 1 vol. 16mo. $1.00.

CHARLES SPRAGUE'S WRITINGS. 75 cents.

OAKFIELD. A Novel. By Lieut. Arnold. $1.00.

A PHYSICIAN'S VACATION. By Dr. Walter Channing. $1.50.

POEMS AND PARODIES. By Phœbe Cary. 75 cents.

LIFE OF EDMUND BURKE. By James Prior. 2 vols. $2.00.

CHURCH AND CONGREGATION. By C. A. Bartol. $1.00.

POEMS. By Matthew Arnold. 75 cents.

POEMS. By Fanny Kemble. Enlarged Edition. $1.00.

ADVENTURES OF TYLL OWLGLASS. $2.50.

LYRIC POEMS, &c. By George Lunt. Cloth. 63 cents.

THREE ERAS OF NEW ENGLAND. By George Lunt. $1.00.

JULIA. A Poem. By George Lunt. 50 cents.

THE MYSTIC, AND OTHER POEMS. By P. J. Bailey. 50 cents.

THE ANGEL WORLD, &c. By P. J. Bailey. 50 cents.

THE AGE, A SATIRE. By P. J. Bailey. 75 cents.
A JOURNEY DUE NORTH. By G. A. Sala. $1.00.
POEMS. By Paul H. Hayne. 1 vol. 16mo. 63 cents.
AVOLIO. By Paul H. Hayne. 1 vol. 75 cents.
SEED-GRAIN. By Mrs. A. C. Lowell. 2 vols. $1.75.
EDUCATION OF GIRLS. By Mrs. A. C. Lowell. 25 cents.
THE PRESERVATION OF HEALTH, &c. By Dr. John C. Warren. 1 vol. 38 cents.
LIFE OF DR. JOHN C. WARREN. By Edward Warren, M. D. Compiled chiefly from his Private Journals. 2 vols. 8vo. $3.50.

In Blue and Gold.

LONGFELLOW'S POETICAL WORKS. 2 vols. $1.75.
do. PROSE WORKS. 2 vols. $1.75.
TENNYSON'S POETICAL WORKS. 1 vol. 75 cents.
WHITTIER'S POETICAL WORKS. 2 vols. $1.50.
LEIGH HUNT'S POETICAL WORKS. 2 vols. $1.50.
GERALD MASSEY'S POETICAL WORKS. 1 vol. 75 cents.
MRS. JAMESON'S CHARACTERISTICS OF WOMEN. 75 cts.
do. DIARY OF AN ENNUYÉE. 1 vol. 75 cts.
do. LOVES OF THE POETS. 1 vol. 75 cts.
do. SKETCHES OF ART, &c. 1 vol. 75 cts.
do. STUDIES AND STORIES. 1 vol. 75 cts.
do. ITALIAN PAINTERS. 1 vol. 75 cents.
do. LEGENDS OF THE MADONNA. 1 vol. 75 cents.
OWEN MEREDITH'S POEMS. 1 vol. 75 cents.
do. LUCILE: A Poem. 1 vol. 75 cents.
BOWRING'S MATINS AND VESPERS. 1 vol. 75 cents.
LOWELL'S (J. RUSSELL) POETICAL WORKS. 2 vols. $1.50.
PERCIVAL'S POETICAL WORKS. 2 vols. $1.75.
MOTHERWELL'S POEMS. 1 vol. 75 cents.
SYDNEY DOBELL'S POEMS. 1 vol. 75 cents.
WILLIAM ALLINGHAM'S POEMS. 1 vol. 75 cents.
HORACE. Translated by Theodore Martin. 1 vol. 75 cts.

www.ingramcontent.com/pod-product-compliance
Lightning Source LLC
LaVergne TN
LVHW020236110826
845151LV00003B/935

* 9 7 8 1 4 2 5 5 3 1 1 5 7 *